Herman Wesley Small

A History of Swan's Island, Maine

Herman Wesley Small

A History of Swan's Island, Maine

ISBN/EAN: 9783744733724

Printed in Europe, USA, Canada, Australia, Japan

Cover: Foto ©ninafisch / pixelio.de

More available books at **www.hansebooks.com**

A HISTORY

OF

SWAN'S ISLAND,

MAINE.

BY

H. W. SMALL, M. D.

ELLSWORTH, ME.:
HANCOCK COUNTY PUBLISHING COMPANY, PRINTERS.
1898.

TABLE OF CONTENTS.

CHAPTER.		PAGE.
I.	Introduction—Aborigines—Discovery,	3
II.	Purchase — Settlement and Land Titles,	17
III.	A Sketch of the Life of Col. James Swan,	44
IV.	Biographical Sketches of Early Settlers,	59
V.	Gott's Island,	159
VI.	The Fishing Industry,	175
VII.	Synopsis of the Municipal Records,	204
VIII.	Miscellaneous,	233

HISTORY OF SWAN'S ISLAND.

CHAPTER I.

INTRODUCTION—ABORIGINES—DISCOVERY.

UPON the very threshold of this historical sketch I found myself quite destitute of early public records. For over half a century from the settlement of this island until its organization as a plantation no municipal records were kept. But I have been fortunate in bringing to light many private family records, old deeds showing what lots were occupied by the pioneer settlers; and written mutual agreements, which seem to have been often the result of arbitration on any disputed point where different claims to land conflicted with one another.

A great deal of the information which I have received concerning the early settlers was obtained from the oldest inhabitants of the island, many of whom were children of the first settlers, and in a few instances the latter of the pioneer settlers themselves. In this part, which I have obtained from the memory of aged people, some errors may appear, but in the main it will be found correct, as a great deal of pains has been taken to verify these records.

I feel that no apology is necessary for occasionally going beyond the limits of this town and bringing in the sketch of some person directly connected with the family under consideration, for a book of this kind must necessarily be excursive in its character.

All the subjects of the following biographical sketches have been candidly and impartially treated, nothing withheld that would be of public interest, nor praise bestowed where it is undeserved. I think that everything of importance which has transpired here since its settlement, over a century ago, that would be of public interest, has been here recorded. I have thought best to gain and preserve this historical knowledge before the source from which it could be obtained is gone, when it would have been lost forever. It should be a matter of interest to all of us to preserve a record of our ancestors. These hardy pioneers came to this "island of the sea", cleared the unbroken forests, cultivated farms, built their houses, reared their families, and made it possible for their children to have advantages which they never possessed. Whatever of comforts or of ~~luxuries~~ that we now enjoy is due, in a great measure, to them as a result of their labor. They sowed the seed amid great privation and toil, and we are reaping the harvest. So it is most fitting that their names should ever be held in grateful memory by their descendants.

The location of Swan's Island is in Hancock county, thirty-six miles south of Ellsworth, and is separated from Mount Desert by four miles of water. The island proper contains 5,875 acres, besides a number of smaller islands which are included in the town. It is entirely surrounded by the Atlantic ocean, yet several islands intervene between it and the open sea. The surface contains no great eminences, but is generally hilly. The ocean has made great indentations into the island, cutting it into great peninsulas which, in some instances, nearly unite, the enclosure forming excellent harbors which offer safe shelter to vessels of the largest size. Excellent crops reward those who till the soil, yet on account of the rocky nature of the land, farming was never carried out to any great extent. An inexhaustible supply of granite forms the southern part of the island, but the fishing business now, as ever in the past, is the leading industry.

The remote history of this island, like that of all America, is shrouded in darkness. I am not able to raise the curtain and look into the past and see the people whom we know, by unmistakable traces, made their homes here, reared their young, carried on their ancient mode of hunting and fishing as a means of subsistence. Here, too, they died; and when the white men came to take possession of these ancient hunting grounds, they found only the ruins of savage occupancy. This was undoubtedly a favorite resort for the red men. The cool bracing atmosphere of the island tempted them to leave the seclusion of their forest homes, especially during the warmer months of the year. This island then furnished excellent hunting grounds. Sea fowl came in great flocks so near that they could be easily killed by their rude weapons, besides the excellent fishing in the harbor or very near the shore made it practicable to use their birch bark canoes. Also in winter the severity of the weather often drove them to the seashore to secure shell fish for food when all other sources were cut off. In some parts of the island where the primitive forest was cleared and the soil first broken by the plow, the ground for very large spaces would be literally whitened with the remains of Indian dinners. Under huge trees that perhaps had been standing hundreds of years clam shell would be found to great depth in the ground.

In 1614 when Capt. John Smith first visited these shores the number of Indians within the limits of the present State of Maine was estimated at 30,000. The tribe that occupied this section was the Tarratines, the remnant of whom now resides at Oldtown and at present numbers 446. These Indians were noted for the long distances they went in their canoes, and this gave to them the general name of Etechmins.

At that part of the island called the "North" when the first settlers came there were five different places plainly seen where the Indians had their "set-downs" or villages. There was another at the Middle Head, one in the Reed field near the eastern shore, and several around Old Harbor. In these ancient shell heaps have been found, by men of our present day, flint arrow heads and hatchets which must have taken much skill and patience in making. These must have been their implements used in hunting and perhaps in warfare. The promontory where the light-house stands, near the entrance to Old Harbor, is called Hocomock, a name given to it by the Indians long before the white men came. It may have been their name for this locality. Near to Hocomock Head is a point of land extending into the harbor, called Burying Point. A large number of Indian skeletons were unearthed by the plow. They were found most plenty near the Middle Head and near the "Carrying-place", which places were their burying-grounds. The skeletons were found just beneath the turf and were of large size, showing a race of much larger stature than the Indian of today. This tribe made irregular visits to the island for many years after the white settlers came, but of late, since their number has so decreased, they have ceased altogether.

DISCOVERY.

The first European who visited this island is not known. The first authentic record was made by Champlain during his voyage along this coast in 1604. He made a map of the whole coast and gave the names to many of the islands on either side of us, such as Isle au Haut, Mount Desert, Petit Plaisants, etc.; many of these names, which show their French origin, are still retained. Champlain gave the name of this island on that early map as Brule-cote, "brule" meaning burnt, and "cote" hill— Burnt-hill. It is supposed that Champlain designated the island by some hill that had been burnt over. Some later discoverer translated "brule" burnt, but did not translate "cote", hence on his map he incorrectly gave this island the name Burnt Cote. Another, more stupid still, thought the former had made a mistake in spelling, and on *his* map had *Burn* Coat, by which name it is called in a deed given October 28, 1790, as recorded in Hancock registry, book 1, page 28. Later it was generally known as Burnt Coat or Burnt Coal Island.

It is quite probable that Champlain visited and explored this island, as would seem likely by the accurate map he drew of this and the neighboring islands. That some earlier explorer even than Champlain visited this island seems likely, as he found a portion of the island burned over. Perhaps the settlers on Mount Desert may have made a harbor here while out on their fishing cruises, but no other traces of habitation of the white man were left. Traditional accounts say that the Northmen visited all this region even as early as 1008. But if true, they left no traces here to remind us of their visit.

Mount Desert seems to have been resorted to by European discoverers at a very early date, probably for the reason that its hills can be seen some sixty miles at sea, thus making it a prominent landmark. In 1556 Andrew Trevit, a Catholic priest, sailed in a French ship along the coast. He landed and had many conferences with the natives, among whom he tried to establish the Roman Catholic religion, but we do not learn that he met with any success. There was great rivalry in Europe about this time between the Catholics and Protestants in spreading their respective faiths into new lands.

The French sent De Monte in 1602 to further explore these islands and adjacent mainland, which he took possession of in the name of the king of France, and in true Catholic style set up a cross and called the land he discovered "Acadie", by which name all this region was known until the capture of Quebec by General Wolf in 1759.

The French again passed this island and went to Mount Desert and established the first Jesuit mission in America in 1604.

The patent of Acadia to De Monte was, two years later, surrendered to Madame de Guercheville. This lady was a zealous Catholic and wished to convert the Indians to that faith. Her colony landed on Mount Desert on May 16, 1613, where they built a fort, erected a cross, celebrated mass, and founded a convent. They named the place Saint Sauveur. The French, as we have seen, were getting a strong foothold in this region, but the English Protestants, in the meantime, had not been idle.

In 1603 Capt. George Weymouth visited these shores. He found a great number of Indians on the shores with whom he carried on a brisk trade, receiving rich furs in exchange for worthless baubles which pleased the savage mind. He took possession of the land he visited in the name of the English sovereign. Weymouth was treated with kindness by the Indians, but their friendship was rewarded by kidnapping five of their number, and carrying them to England, three of whom he delivered to Sir Ferdenand Gorges, who in 1639 received a royal charter of the Province of Maine.

The next Englishman of whom we have record who visited this coast was Capt. John Smith, of Virginia, in 1614. He sailed along and explored the coast of Maine with the intention of forming a settlement. He reported having found a settlement, which was the French at Mount Desert. So he must have come very near this island, if he did not explore it; for it is separated from Mount Desert by only four miles of water.

Smith built several boats during the summer, thus becoming the pioneer ship-builder of Maine. Some of his men were engaged in fishing; others more thoroughly explored the coast. Late in the summer Smith returned to England in one of his ships, while another, in charge of Thomas Hunt, tarried behind, captured thirty Indians who were carried to Malaga and sold into slavery. Thus we see that in nearly every instance the Englishmen rewarded the trusting and child-like simplicity of the Indians by some act of treachery. This, no doubt, was the cause of the hatred which the Indians had against the English settlers.

The French, on the other hand, held out the olive branch to the simple natives. They established missionary stations among them. The Indians took kindly to the Catholic faith, and ever after became the faithful allies of the French.

Various Europeans visited this coast for trading and fishing. Hundreds of vessels, even at this early date, visited the waters from Newfoundland to Cape Cod. The entire coast was dotted with temporary habitations for the accommodation of the fishermen. We do not know that there were any permanent settlements here during the voyages of these European discoverers, but there is no doubt that Old Harbor was frequented by fishermen from the neighboring settlements on account of the excellent harbor it afforded, and so conveniently near the fishing grounds. Fishing must at this time have been the leading occupation of the inhabitants of all the seaboard towns, and, in fact, led to their settlement.

In the year 1688, the French king gave to a French gentleman named Cadilliac a tract of land in Acadia embracing the whole of Mount Desert and a large strip of mainland, and all the islands in front of this on the seaboard. He held it until 1713, styling himself Lord of Donaqua and Mount Desert. After the Revolution, one M. Gregoire claimed the whole island for his wife, Maria T., granddaughter of Cadilliac. In consideration of a request made by Lafayette in favor of the Gregoires' claim, Massachusetts recognized it as valid. This is the only French claim sustained in Maine. The heirs of Cadilliac, therefore, received a quit-claim deed of 60,000 acres on the mainland: this included the present towns of Trenton, Lamoine, Sullivan, Ellsworth, Eden and Mount Desert.

In 1754 Spain joined France in a declaration of war against England. As soon as it was heard of in America their respective countrymen took up the quarrel here. The Indians of Canada and Maine aided the French, and for long years this sparsely-settled country was the scene of much bloodshed and distress from want. This was the final struggle in America for supremacy between the French Catholics and the English Protestants.

The French claim was founded on the discovery of the coast by Verrazzano in 1524, on the discovery and occupancy of Canada by Cartier in 1535, on the grant of Henry IV to De Monte, and on the voyages and discoveries of Champlain. The English based their claim on the discovery by Cabot, in possessing Newfoundland by Gilbert in 1553, and by the voyages of discovery of Gosnold, Pring and Weymouth, by the royal charter of 1606, by the occupancy of the country by Popham, and subsequently by Gorges and others.

In 1755 an expedition of two thousand men was sent to drive all the French from Acadia. This movement was demanded by the English governor, Lawrence. When this army arrived, it was placed under the command of Lieutenant-colonel Monkton, who added to his own number about two hundred and seventy regulars and a small train of artillery. This expedition set out in May, and before the first of September every stronghold in Acadia was in the hands of the English. There were eighteen thousand inhabitants of French extraction who, though by the treaty between France and England, were considered neutral, yet were indissolubly attached to the nation from which they sprang. They took no part in all the wars, but they secretly afforded aid, harbor and recruits to the enemy, so the resident authorities demanded that those about the Basin of Minas and in Cumberland county adjoining should be removed. Accordingly nearly two thousand of them were transported and distributed along the coast from Maine to Florida. Upon this event was founded the beautiful poem "Evangeline", by H. W. Longfellow. Constant warfare was thus kept up, inflicting severe injury to all the inhabitants of Maine, until the fall of Quebec in 1759, when this country was forever wrested from the domain of France.

The extinction of French authority in this country was the beginning of a new and prosperous era for Maine. Deserted towns were repeopled, new ones sprang up along the coast, and the sound of the woodsman's axe began to be heard in the interior. From this time until the Revolution the tide of immigration set towards Maine, and the progress in wealth and population was marvelous; but the breaking out of the war put a stop to this progress for many years. Those who were preparing to come here went into the army. During the Revolution the inhabitants along the coast suffered severely for their patriotism. The English took Castine, burned Falmouth, now Portland, and harassed and destroyed our fishing and coasting vessels.

The war closed in 1783, after which there was a large accession to the population of Maine—a move from the older states to this newer district whose resources were now beginning to be developed. Soldiers who had served through the war and were now discharged sought homes in these eastern lands. This island was purchased about this time, and many settlers came directly from Massachusetts. In fact, Maine's population is made up almost wholly from the descendants of the settlers in the older states, receiving few foreign emigrants.

The district of Maine in 1783 became a part of Massachusetts and remained under its jurisdiction until Maine became an independent state. Shortly after the close of the Revolution the question of separation came up for discussion, and several towns voted upon it; but as most of the inhabitants were from Massachusetts, their attachment for the old commonwealth was not weakened. In 1787 an effort was again made and carried by so small a majority, and the entire vote was so small, that it was thought best to abandon it for the present. The position of Massachusetts during the war of 1812 in opposing the measures of the President and Congress was highly distasteful to the patriotic inhabitants of Maine, and doubtless influenced voters in bringing about the desired result. Maine was admitted into the Union as an independent state in 1820.

The census of Maine in 1789 showed 96,540 inhabitants: in 1800 there were 151,719, and in 1810 there were 228,334 people. We can thus see how rapidly Maine was becoming populated. Burnt Coat Island, as it was called, was bought by Col. James Swan, of Massachusetts, in the year 1786. Many of the wealthy men of the older states were buying up property in Maine — investments which promised good returns. This island, as well as the other islands included in Col. Swan's purchase, was covered with a valuable forest of timber, which undoubtedly attracted the purchaser. Manufactured lumber found a ready market at the many towns and villages that were building up along the coast. Burnt Coat, at the time of its purchase, was in the county of Lincoln (where many of the early records relating to this island may be found), until Hancock county was formed June 25, 1789.

Hancock county has a more extensive seaboard and more numerous harbors than any other coast of equal extent in the United States. When Massachusetts came into possession of this territory, the mainland was divided into townships and the islands into groups convenient for classifying, such as the Deer Isle group, the Burnt Coat group, the Mount Desert group, etc. The Burnt Coat group extended from Isle au Haut on the west, near Flye's Point on the north, to the Mount Desert group on the east, and the Atlantic ocean on the south.

This territory was offered for sale for three reasons: first, that Massachusetts might derive revenue from its sale; second, to ensure its settlement, and thus increase the state's population; and third, that only Protestants might become owners of this land, and thus prevent the encroachments of the Catholics. This prejudice against the Catholic religion, formed in those times, still exists at the present day.

Usually the conditions that Massachusetts imposed were: if granted a township six miles square, that it should be settled by sixty Protestant families within six years, and each family have a house at least eighteen feet square; to fit for tillage three hundred acres of land, and erect a meeting-house and settle a pastor.

Col. Swan, soon after the purchase of these islands, erected a saw and a grist mill. He built a store and erected for himself a large mansion, which he finished up in a most expensive manner. Many of the wealthy men of that day still favored the English custom of owning large estates; this was seen especially in the great plantations of the South. This seems to have been Swan's object.

They began at the saw mill to manufacture the great logs, which at first were cut near the shore and rafted to the mill. The grist mill manufactured the barley and corn, which the settlers were now raising on their cleared land, for bread. Coasting vessels were being built to carry the lumber to market, and return laden with supplies for the settlers. The woodman's axe and the carpenter's hammer were heard on every side. New houses grew as if by magic. Everything for the new settlement was now in readiness. The mills were in operation. Settlers with their families were rapidly accepting the lucrative employment which was here offered them, and all indications promised this to be one of the most thriving towns of the East.

CHAPTER II.

PURCHASE, SETTLEMENT AND LAND TITLES.

The following is the agreement, deed and receipt of payment for the Burnt Coat group of islands, between the Commonwealth of Massachusetts and James Swan. These interesting documents, which show what islands were included in the original purchase, were found in the Lincoln county records, in which county this group of islands was then included.

COMMONWEALTH OF MASSACHUSETTS.

THIS AGREEMENT made this twenty-fifth day of February, A. D. 1785, between the Committee appointed by a Resolve of the General Court of the twenty-eighth of October, A. D. 1783, on the subject of unappropriated Lands in the County of Lincoln, in behalf of this Commonwealth, of the one part, and James Swan, of Dorchester, in the County of Suffolk, Esq., of the other part.

WITNESSETH, that the said Committee do agree to sell and convey to the said James Swan, to hold in fe, a certain Island commonly known by the name of Burnt Coat Island, in the said County of Lincoln, and all the Islands, the center thereof are within three miles of any part of the said Burnt Coat Island, and a good Deed thereof to be given to the said James Swan as soon as the same Islands can be conveniently surveyed and a return thereof had. And the said James Swan agrees on his part to pay on the nineteenth Day of March next, the sum of nineteen hundred and twenty Pounds in the consolidated securities of this Commonwealth to said committee, to the Use of said Commonwealth, and the further sum of three shillings in the said securities per Acre for every Acre that shall be found to be contained in the said Islands over and above the number of twelve thousand eight hundred acres (to be paid for by the first said Payment) on an accurate survey thereof in one year from this date. Any Islands the whole thereof is a barren rock, to be excepted, but no allowance to be made for any Bogs, Ponds, or waste Lands, and on the delivery of said Deed to give satisfactory securities for the said last mentioned Payment. In witness thereof the parties aforesaid set their hands the day and year first above mentioned.

S. PHILLIPS, JR.,
NATHAN DANE,
JAMES SWAN,
SAMUEL PAGE,
Committee.

RECEIPT.

March, 19, 1785.

Received of James Swan, Esq., the first within mentioned sum of Nineteen hundred and twenty Pounds.

NATHAN DANE.

January 19, 1786.

Received of the hon'ble Samuel Phillips, Esqr., the above sum, which was overpaid on the within Lands purchased of the Commonwealth of Massachusetts, say one hundred and twenty Pounds.

JAMES SWAN.

DEED.

KNOW ALL MEN BY THESE PRESENTS,

That We, Samuel Phillips, Jun., Nathaniel Wells and John Brooks, Esquires, a committee appointed by two Resolves of the Commonwealth of Massachusetts of the 28th of October, 1783 and 30th of November, 1785, on the subject of unappropriated Lands in the County of Lincoln, and by those and other Resolves of said Court, empowered to sell and convey the unappropriated Lands of the said Commonwealth in said County, for and in consideration of the sum of one thousand four hundred and forty-three Pounds, nine shillings, in the consolidated securities of said Commonwealth, to us paid by James Swan, of Boston, in the County of Suffolk and Commonwealth aforesaid, Esquires, have given, granted, bargained, sold and conveyed and by these presents in behalf of the said Commonwealth do give, grant, bargain, sell and convey unto the said James Swan, his Heirs and assigns, the following Islands lying and being in the County of Lincoln and Commonwealth aforesaid, and scituated southerly and southeastly of a Point of main Land known by the name of Naskig Point, being the southeastly Point of N IV Township between the Penobscot River and Union River granted by the General Court of the late Province of Massachusetts Bay, to David Marsh and others, on the second Day of March, one thousand seven hundred and sixty-two, and southwestly of the Island called Mount Desert, viz.:

Burnt Coat or Burnt Coal Island, containing five thousand eight hundred and seventy-five acres; Island P, sixteen Acres; Island I, six acres 57 Rods; Island K five acres, 136 Rods; John's Island twenty Acres, 10 Rods; Island N, twenty-three Acres, 64 Rods; Island B, four Acres; Hatt Island, twenty Acres; Harbour Island, one hundred forty-four Acres, 16 Rods; Marshal's Island, eight hundred forty-three Acres, 80 Rods; Little Marshal Island, forty-two Acres, 40 Rods; Island W, ten Acres; Island A, twenty-one Acres; Island C, forty-four Acres, 60 Rods; Island D, sixteen Acres; Island F, twenty Acres; Island G, thirty-three Acres; Loud Island, one thousand one hundred thirty-two Acres, 130 Rods; Pond Island, two hundred and seven Acres; Island U, seventeen Acres, 100 Rods; Island V, three Acres; Westly Calf Island, two hundred fifty-six Acres, 140 Rods; Eastern Calf Island, one hundred sixty-two Acres, 80 Rods; all of which Islands belong to and comprise the Division of Islands called Burnt Coat division, surveyed for the Commonwealth, aforesaid, Anno Domini, 1785, according to a Plan thereof, returned into the aforesaid committee's office by Rufus Putnam and entered in the Plan Book, page 118, in which Plan the several Islands aforesaid, with their Magnitudes, Bearings and distances from each other, as well as from Naskig Point are laid down, which Division of Islands are separated from other Islands and bounded as follows, viz.: Southerly by the Atlantic Ocean; Westley by Jerico Bay, which separates them from Isle of Holt and Deer Island Division, Northerly by a line drawn due East from the southern extreme of Naskig Point into Placentia Bay, which Bay divides them from the Great Placentia Islands, and other islands lying Southerly of Mount Desert. Also two other Islands lying Easterly of Placentia Bay, aforesaid, surveyed and included in Mount Desert Division of Islands, entered in the aforesaid Plan Book, Page 132, viz.: Great Placentia Island containing four hundred forty-seven Acres, 155 Rods; and is scituated Northeastly of said Burnt Coat Island about three hundred and seventy rods, and Black Island, containing two hundred ninety-two Acres, 55 Rods, lying southerly of Great Placentia Island and distance therefrom about two hundred and forty Rods. Both of these as well as all the other Islands before described being within three miles of some part or other of the great Island first mentioned.

The before described Islands containing in the Whole, Nine thousand, six hundred twenty-three acres and three rods by Measure, according to the several

Plans of the same in the aforesaid Committee's office, Togather with the rights Members Profits Priviledges and Appurtenances whatsoever, thereunto belonging, or in any wise appertaining. To have and to hold the said bargained and granted Premises with the Appurtenances unto him, the said Swan, his Heirs and Assigns to his and their proper Use, and behoof forever. And the said Committee, in behalf of said Commonwealth covenant and agree with said Swan, his Heirs and Assigns, that at the Time of ensealing thereof the said Commonwealth of Massachusetts is seized and possessed of said granted Premises in fee, and that they, the said Samuel Phillips, Junr., Nathaniel Wells, and John Brooks, have good Right in their said Capacities and in behalf of said Commonwealth to sell and convey the same in manner aforesaid, the Premises being free of all Incumberances, and that the said Commonwealth shall warrant and defend the same granted Premises, to the said James Swan, his Heirs and Assigns forever against the lawful claims and Demands of all Persons.

In witness whereof the said Committee hereto, set their hands and seals this seventh Day of July, in the year of our Lord, one thousand seven hundred and eighty-six. SAMUEL PHILLIPS, JUNR. [seal]
NATH'L WELLS. [seal]
J. BROOKS. [seal]

Signed, sealed and delivered in presence of
LEONARD JARVIS.
GEO. R. MINOT.

SUFFOLK SS. July 7, 1786.
Then the within named Samuel Phillips, Junr., Nath'l Wells and John Brooks personally appeared and acknowledged the before written Instrument by each of them signed to be their free Act and Deed, before me.
STEPHEN METCALF,
Justice of the Peace.

SETTLEMENT.

When this island was discovered by Europeans, it was, as before stated, entirely covered with a dense forest of hardwood trees. The trees of this primitive forest attained great size, as was shown by the enormous stumps found throughout the forest by the older inhabitants. This luxuriant growth was, no doubt, due to the large amount of foliage decaying, thus fertilizing the soil. After the first growth was cut off, the land was burned over. This was injurious to the soil where it covered rocky land, and much of its richness was washed into the valleys and thence into the ocean. The next growth on this impoverished soil was much smaller. This can be remembered by many of the older inhabitants.

When this forest was, in turn, cleared, its place was taken by a stunted growth of spruce and fir trees, which now covers a part of the island. The first forest is what attracted the attention of the people from the more populated districts. Lumber was then in great demand to meet the wants of the growing towns and villages along the coast; and to meet these wants, Swan erected a sawmill to manufacture the lumber. This wood also found a ready market as fuel, it being before coal came into use: and although it brought but a small price, often selling for fifty cents per cord on the bank, yet it grew so abundantly near the shore that fair wages could be made. It was the chief employment of the men during the winter months.

At an early date quite a colony of Irishmen completely cut off the wood from that part of the island since called Irish Point, this giving to it the name.

After Swan's purchase, his first work was to build a dam across the mill-pond and erect his mills. The location was on either side of the little island, near where the lobster factory was afterwards built. He built a sawmill over the stream on one side of the island, and a gristmill on the other. He then built a large mansion which he proceeded to finish up in excellent style. This house was built in colonial style of architecture, the roof being almost flat. This was called by the settlers the "Big House". It was located near the shores of Old Harbor, below where Harvey Bridges now lives.

The state of Massachusetts agreed to exempt Swan's property from taxation for a period of twenty years, provided he settled, within seven years, twenty-two Protestant families on the island, built or caused to be built twenty-two houses at least twenty-two feet square, and built a church and school-house and established a grammar school.

In order to get the required number of settlers, Swan sent out to the surrounding towns that he would give one hundred acres of land to any settler who would bring his family, build a house, cultivate the land, and that, at the end of seven years, he would give him a deed, free of expense, for the land which he had so improved.

Quite a number of families came from Deer Isle, Sedgwick, Mount Desert and other places. There was a great demand for laborers. Many found employment at the mills. A large number chopped logs in the forest, others with ox teams drew them to the mill where they were manufactured into lumber. Many coasters from other places came to take the lumber to market, and Old Harbor took on a lively aspect.

Some of the early settlers made their first visit here in

one of these coasting vessels. In the meantime the fishery business began to be developed. But few were employed in this industry at first, for other occupations were more lucrative. In after years, however, the fishery business came to be the chief employment of the whole town. The church and school-house were never built, as Swan, soon after his purchase here, failed in business and left this country before it could be carried into effect, and those into whose hands the property fell did not choose to fulfill Swan's agreement.

Swan had as a confidential agent a man named Joseph Prince, of Beverly, Massachusetts. He came here soon after the purchase of the islands and superintended Swan's business during the early days of their settlement. Prince received $500 a year and his family supported. He settled on Harbor Island and built a house near the cove which still bears his name. Hancock registry, volume 5, page 481, gives the following account, dated February 28, 1798: James Swan, of Dorchester, appointed Joseph Prince resident on Swan's Island, formerly Burntcoat (this is the first time that the phrase Swan's Island was used), with power of attorney to sell and convey to David Smith, Joshua Grindle and Moses Staples one hundred acres of land each; to John Rich, William Davis, David Bickmore, Isaac Sawyer, and —— Knowlton thirty acres each, all to be taken on the Great Island; and to Samuel Emerson sixty acres on Marshall's Island, and to any other fisherman, who owns his fishing boat and who may settle on the Great Island, ten acres. To be theirs on the following conditions only: They shall live on said land seven years, counting from their actual settlement, with their stock and families; shall pay all the taxes assessed by the town, State or general government; they shall cut no more wood or timber than to make good and farmerlike improvements; shall pay the expense of surveying; each shall lay out such roads through his land as the agent shall direct, and keep it in repair seven years.

As far as the case may admit, the cord wood and lumber cut upon these lands shall be carried to market in vessels belonging to Swan or his heirs. In like manner the logs felled on this land shall be carried to the mills erected or to be erected on said island. If the above conditions are not complied with, the land that may be improved by settlers will go back to said Swan. This was acknowledged in Boston before John Vinal.

Soon after the year 1800, Prince moved back to Beverly. His widow was living there as late as 1841, a very aged lady. They have many descendants now living in Beverly and Salem. After Prince's departure, Swan's business was transacted by different parties, as will be noted later. Swan's property was now neglected. The mills, which still ran for many years, were finally closed and gradually fell into decay.

The land was held as of very little value after the timber had been cut off, and settlers who came in made their own selection of lots without consulting anyone. The first permanent settlement was made by David Smith in 1791. He settled on Harbor Island, where his daughter Sarah, afterwards the wife of Benjamin Stinson, was born in 1792. He soon after moved into the "Big House" while building his own, and while there, his son Benjamin Smith was born in 1795. This is said to be the first child born to white parents on the island.

The "Big House" was used as a temporary dwelling by many of the early settlers until a suitable house of their own could be procured. Although there were sawmills here, most of the first houses were built of logs. The crevices were plastered with mortar made from burnt clam shells. These were found in large quantities, and made a good substitute for lime. Moses Staples made considerable quantity in this way when he lived near Old Harbor.

The log houses were small, generally twenty-two feet square; the lower part was all in one room called the "kitchen". This was used as a cook-room, dining-room, sitting-room, store-room and general workshop. It was the family "home", and very often here large families were reared. The largest of which we have record is David Smith's, before spoken of, who by his first wife had sixteen children, and by his second wife eight, making twenty-four in all.

In the kitchen was a broad fireplace wherein swung a large crane. Upon the crane were pendant hooks of various lengths, upon which the pots and kettles were hung. There was a wide, neatly-swept hearth, upon which, before a roaring fire, the bright tin baker was placed to bake the bread or roast the lamb. When a bannock was to be baked, the dough of corn-meal and water was spread about an inch thick upon a piece of sheet iron about eight by eighteen inches, and placed upon the hearth-edge and a flatiron at its back to keep it up. When its face side was cooked which, with a winter fire, required only a few minutes, it was removed from the iron, turned inside out and again presented to the fire for a few minutes. That gave it a hard, brittle crust on both sides. These bannocks of corn or barley were the only bread used. Wheat flour was very expensive, and could be used only by the more wealthy.

At the side of the fireplace, and quite near thereto, was a cavernous oven which each Saturday was heated very hot, where the Sunday's beans and brown bread and pumpkin pies, or a quarter of lamb were baked. Under the oven was the stock-hole, with a capacity of several barrels, into which the ashes from the hearth were shoveled.

In autumn, after the harvest had been gathered and the house banked and all cracks and crannies about the house and barn where Jack Frost might come in were properly tightened to keep him out, it was the correct thing to lay in a supply of pitch wood for winter evenings' light.

The furniture was of the simplest description. Spinning wheels and looms manufactured the wool into cloth which served largely to clothe the family.

During the long, bleak winters, shut off from all communication with the main land, except an occasional sail-boat, with the waves of the Atlantic ocean beating all around them, it must, indeed, have seemed isolated. But it was not so regarded by them. The little log house was built in a sheltered spot in the forest. The sturdy settler, to support his large family, was kept busy throughout the day. In the evening the family gathered before the fire in the huge fireplace, whose genial warmth gave a cheery aspect to the little cabin. During the evening friends would come with their family hauled by oxen, perhaps for several miles. The younger members would entertain themselves by coasting or skating or by games within doors, while with the parents story-telling seems to have been a favorite mode of entertainment, in which a ghost or a goblin would figure as the hero of the tale. A generous supper would be partaken of before they left for their long ride homeward. Notwithstanding the great improvements that have taken place within the last century, I doubt if people enjoy themselves now more than they did at that time. An increase of means brings with it one of wants, and usually the expenditures will keep pace with the income.

Many of the more prosperous soon built timber houses, some of large dimensions. Most of the houses were built near the shore so as to be convenient for fishing, which, since the departure of Swan's agents, had been their chief reliance for the support of their families. The first work of the settler, after providing for his family, was to procure a boat. These were of small size at first, as an abundance of fish could be caught near the shore, but after a time larger boats and vessels were built, not only for home use but also to sell. Land was cleared around the house and barley, corn and potatoes were raised. Barley and corn were ground at the gristmill and made into bread.

Although farming was never carried on to any great extent, crops were good. It is said that some of the farmers raised a thousand bushels of potatoes per year.

A large amount of kiln wood was sold during the winter months. At first this wood could be cut anywhere except on land actually settled. Later the plantation required a small price per cord on all wood cut on wild lands. Fish were plenty, but they brought a small price. Yet they served as an article of food, and were exchanged for corn, barley, and articles of clothing. Shoes of a rude kind were made at home. The settlers at once stocked their places with cattle and sheep, the latter being more profitable on account of the dry, hilly pasture-land.

There were no roads, only paths through the woods. If any one wished the use of a road he had to build it himself. On account of the rocky character of the land through which roads must pass, they preferred, when visiting another part of the island, to go in boats, rather than incur the heavy expense necessary to construct roads. Later, paths were converted into wood-roads, and these at a much later date into highways, all of which had gates across them. No horses were kept for seventy years after the settlement of the town. But the roads at this writing have vastly improved, in fact, none better can be found in the county.

During the long bleak winters hunting was a favorite pastime. Game was abundant, but so many hunters came from other places that it became necessary for the inhabitants to pass a vote not to allow non-residents trapping, hounding or laying poison for any fur-bearing animal; and still later no man was allowed to hound game except upon his own premises.

Among the fur-bearing animals found here by the settlers were quite a number of bears, some of which were so bold as to come to the barns and eat the food put out for the hogs, and nights they would often prowl around the houses to secure anything left around the door that would tempt their appetite. Two bears were killed here by personal encounters. The first was killed by Abel E. Staples. A large party of men, as was customary in those days, gathered at John Cook's place to assist him in clearing his lot of the bushes and stumps, so as to enable him to cultivate the soil. While so employed, several dogs, which had accompanied the workmen, began to bark furiously in the forest near them. Soon, much to the surprise of all, they drove a large bear into the clearing. The bear made a desperate attempt to escape by attacking those who surrounded him. At this, Mr. Staples, using a long stick which he had been using prying stumps, struck the bear on the head. This only enraged the beast the more. The second blow, given with tremendous force, split open the bear's head, and he fell over dead. A long time subsequent, a bear came out on the shore where John and David Stinson were working on a boat near their home at the north. One of the brothers started for the house to get a rifle, while the other kept watch. Presently the bear began to move towards the woods, when Mr. Smith seized a broken oar that lay near his boat, and after a severe battle came off victorious. Several other bears were killed with firearms. This game was so persistently hunted that it was entirely exterminated.

There were also large flocks of seabirds which served as food, and the feathers were made into beds. Seabirds still come in large flocks at certain seasons of the year.

There were no traders then on the island, but supplies were usually laid in before winter. The mails came occasionally, when a boat went to the mainland, but there was no office here nor any regular place to receive the mails.

The war of 1812 made itself felt among the few settlers here, not only in the depression incident to warfare, but the British cutters harassed our coasting vessels and captured and detained many of the fishing vessels, taking from these vessels any man whom they chose to regard as a British subject and impressing him on board of an English ship-of-war. In a similar way the father of Moses Staples, who came here in 1793, was impressed on board of a British war ship during the Revolution. He was never heard of after that, and probably died or was killed while in the service.

It is related that while one of the British cutters was near our harbor, a boat came ashore, and her crew espied several women and girls returning in a boat from one of the islands where they had been berrying. The cutter's boat went in pursuit, and soon overtook the party of frightened women. They, however, did not detain them, but on leaving them an officer in the boat kissed one of the young girls. "Go home," said he, "and tell your parents that you have had the honor of being kissed by a British officer."

In the year 1810, just previous to our second war with Great Britain, an embargo was laid on flour to prevent it being exported to England or to the English colonies. Accordingly flour in Canada brought a very high price, and made smuggling into that country profitable. So in this year, two brothers named Prudy, who were Tories, brought a load of flour in a Chebacco boat, and stored it in the cellar of the "Big House", awaiting a favorable opportunity to smuggle it into Canada, but some patriotic citizen, knowing the character and business of the Prudy boys, notified the customs officer at Deer Isle, who came and, with the aid of David Smith, took charge of the flour, put it on board of a vessel and carried it to Deer Isle, where it was confiscated. The Prudy boys were naturally enraged, especially with Mr. Smith, whom they accused of betraying them to the customs officer. One day, meeting Mr. Smith alone, they both attacked him, but, much to their surprise, this old Revolutionary hero administered to them a sound thrashing, which all of that class so richly deserved. Prudy had Mr. Smith arrested for assault. He was carried to Deer Isle for trial, and, strangely enough, he came for trial before the very customs officer who had made the seizure, and by whom Mr. Smith was discharged on the ground that he was justified in the act as the means of self-defense.

Swan's Island Plantation was organized in 1834. Previously there had been no municipal organization, and had been taxed only by the State. In State and national elections it was classed with Mount Desert, later with Bluehill, and now with Deer Isle. At present Deer Isle, Swan's Island and Isle au Haut form one representative district.

During the first half century after its settlement, there were no public schools, but instruction was furnished the young more or less regularly and supported by private donations. These schools were kept in the room of some dwelling, and the teacher "boarded around". The usual price paid the teacher was nine shillings per week.

The people in those times seem to have made good use of the advantages which were offered them, for most of them had a good common school education. The first school-house was built near the Carrying Place in 1834. This building was afterwards moved and used in district No. 1 until the new school-house was built in 1894. The school-house on the east side was built soon after. The first public winter term of school was taught by Miss Sophia Dodge, of Sedgwick. Among other early teachers were John Adams, Hon. William H. Taylor, a justice of the supreme judicial court of Maine, and Danforth P. Marcyes, of Eden. The wages for a winter teacher was about $14 per month and board, often as low as fifty cents per week. The island was first divided into the west district and east district. In 1839, the east district voted to support school for three months in the summer, and two and a half months in the winter.

In 1842, the west district was divided into two other districts—the southeast district, the line of which was to run between Joseph Gott and John Gott's house, and the Irish Point district, the dividing line to run between Abel Lane's and David Smith's places.

This year the districts were numbered, west district to be known as No. 1, east district as No. 2, southwest district as No. 3, southeast district as No. 4. Later, district No. 1 was again divided; all north of the Carrying Place to be formed into a new district known as No. 5; and last, a portion of district No. 1 was united to a portion of district No. 2, the union forming district No. 6. The last district, however, was soon abolished. The other districts remained until all district lines were abolished by the new school law of 1894.

There were five principal settlements. The most numerous families were the Smiths, Stinsons and Kents at the north; the Joyces, Staples, Torreys and Stockbridges at the east side, the Gotts and Stanleys in No. 1, and the Spragues, Sadlers and Bridges in No. 4. Most of the settlers in each section were related to each other. And a large percentage of the population of this island to-day is descendants of the above-named families.

These people, although surrounded by many disadvantages, have reared a hardy, industrious, intelligent class of people. A general appearance of prosperity prevails. The homes are neat and elegantly furnished. The grounds and lawns are tastefully kept. The roads are kept in a good condition of repair, with sidewalks built in two of the villages. Schools have been liberally supported, offering to the young thirty weeks of instruction in the year. All school-books are furnished free, so that the poor can enjoy equal advantages with the wealthy. A new two-story school-house has just been completed, and the schools for the first time graded (1894).

Seldom has there been a pauper to call for public charity, and the town is without debt.

We of the present day, who now occupy comfortable homes, with all these advantages, with mails and steamboats that daily connect us with the neighboring towns, can scarcely realize the great changes which have taken place for the better within this century.

LAND TITLES.

As we have already seen, the commonwealth of Massachusetts agreed to sell to James Swan the twenty-five islands included in the Burnt Coat group, which were estimated to contain 12,800 acres, at three shillings per acre, which amounted to £1,920. This Swan paid on March 19, 1785, and he was to receive a deed as soon as the islands could be surveyed. By actual measurement this group was found to contain only 9,623 acres, and the difference which Swan overpaid between the estimated and real measure of this group was returned to him January 19, 1789. The deed of this group was given to Swan by the commonwealth on July 7, 1786. On October 28, 1790, James Swan, late of Boston, by his attorneys, Henry Jackson and Benjamin Hitchborn, sold to Joseph Prince, resident of *Burn* Coat, for the sum of £300 "and divers other good causes" Burn Coat Island and all other islands within three miles of said Burn Coat. (1–28) *

After Prince's purchase he followed Swan's agreement with the settlers, by giving a bond to each occupant of the land that he would give him a deed of his property at the end of seven years. To Joseph Toothaker he gave a bond of $100 for the one hundred acres extending from the Carrying Place around the Cove, dated April 26, 1792 (3–208), and to Joshua Grindle for the same amount of land extending from Moses Staples, to the Carrying Place, dated May 1, 1794 (3–245). On June 29, 1795, Joseph Prince and wife Joanna sold to Henry Jackson, of Boston, for £300, the same purchase: on July 16, 1795, (3–256) Jackson also bought of Bartolomy DeGregoire land on Mt. Desert for which he paid £1,247. He also bought Bartlett's island, Cranberry island and Duck island, and also a tract near Stinson's Neck, Deer Isle.

On September 28, 1796, Henry Jackson sold the Burnt Coat group back to Swan in consideration of the sum of £300 (4–206). He also gave Swan a quit-claim deed of these islands and improvments on the same: also

---

* The figures refer to Hancock registry, volume and page, where these records were obtained.

land in Suffolk and Norfolk counties for £5,000 (4-207). On December 6, 1796, Swan mortgaged this property to Henry Jackson to secure the payment of £2,333 (4-203). On July 13, 1798, Swan gave the same security to Stephen Higginson and Samuel G. Perkins, of Boston, as security for $30,000 (5-541). Swan mortgaged this property to other parties at different times to secure payment of loans, all of which were promptly paid.

On February 28, 1798, Swan gave to Joseph Prince, of Swan's Island (formerly Burnt Coat), power of attorney to sell and convey to the settlers the land which they had occupied, and to such other fishermen as might settle, on the conditions which are stated elsewhere. He also gave Prince power to sell a lot of land on "Island of Holt" which Swan had bought of Nathaniel Shelden in 1796. This power of attorney is recorded in (5-481) Hancock registry.

We find no further record that any property here was bought or sold for some fifteen years. During all this time the settlers selected whatever property they choose, and no one disputed their claim. The agreement by which Swan promised the settlers a deed of the property that they occupied at the end of seven years was not carried out by him or by the other parties into whose hands this property fell. It may have been for the reason that when the seven years had expired Swan was in France and had no one here to attend to his business. So the failure may have been due to neglect, or perhaps the settlers did not fulfill the conditions of the contract. However, the settlers did not seem to care much about the title to land that they possessed, which was of very little value. Their log cabins and boats comprised the greater part of their possessions, so if they were ousted their loss would not be very great; besides they considered they had a moral right to the land they occupied, according to Swan's agreement.

On October 3, 1812, "James Swan, of Boston, at present residing in Paris, mortgaged to Michael O'Maley, a merchant of Baltimore," a part of this group of islands. Swan was indebted to O'Maley for the sum of 43,080 francs as appears by a bill of exchange drawn at Harve in 1808. Swan paid on this 6,663 francs with interest, leaving the balance due O'Maley on September 1, 1813, of 36,417 francs. As security Swan mortgaged to O'Maley thirteen islands of this group, viz.: Swan's Island, Marshall's island, Black island, Hat island, Great and Little Placentia islands, Long island " and five others the name not recollected", " containing in all about 12,000 acres, together with the grist and the sawmills, farms, stores, mansion-house, timber lands, waters and fisheries". This mortgage was executed at Paris in the Greffe of the prison of St. Pelagie, where Swan was then imprisoned, and acknowledged before David Bailey Warden, United States consul at Paris, October 3, 1812 (33-226). In this transfer it is noticed that only thirteen of the twenty-five islands included in the Burnt Coat group were conveyed. After this there seems to have been no claimants for this property, either mortgagor or mortgagee, until 1817. During all this time settlers continued to come in and select whatever lots they choose to occupy. unmolested by anyone.

On March 10, 1817, Rufus B. Allyn, of Belfast, as attorney for O'Maley, entered and took peaceable possession of the premises named for the purpose of foreclosing the mortgage. He notified the settlers that in O'Maley's name he should take possession of all this property. He brought as witnesses of this seizure Jesse Holbrook and Paul Giles.

On August 29, 1821, a power of attorney was given by O'Maley to Daniel Webster to transact the business connected with the thirteen islands of the Burnt Coat group, as well as his other transactions with Swan. This was signed by O'Maley in Boston. A power of attorney was given by Swan to William Sullivan (son-in-law) to act jointly with Daniel Webster, they to have the power of substitution, to sell all the islands in this group and execute deeds in their names, and Swan and O'Maley agreed to confirm all acts so transacted. This was dated September 13, 1821.

On June 13, 1823, Daniel Webster, attorney for O'Maley, and William Sullivan, attorney for Swan, substituted Rufus B. Allyn to act jointly for both parties (43–168), and whatever deeds were given afterwards were in Swan and O'Maley's name. As to the mortgage of Swan to O'Maley, it is believed that it was given to a friend to protect the property from other debtors. Swan had considerable property in Boston and vicinity which was conveyed in somewhat the same manner. It is strange that if O'Maley claimed anything under this mortgage he should have waited several years before asserting his claim.

The year after Allyn's appointment he came to these islands and demanded payment of all the settlers for the land which they occupied. He gave to each occupant a deed of the property he occupied, and took a mortgage to secure payment. Both the deeds and mortgages, which are recorded in Hancock registry, were executed between the years 1823 and 1839. The following were given at that time:

Moses Bridges, of Sedgwick, bought Eastern Calf island, containing 162 acres, for $400, May 24, 1823. Mortgage was paid December 5, 1839 (43-509).

Peter Powers bought Western Calf island, containing 256 acres, for $750, September 21, 1822 (43-521).

John Finney bought the place on which he lives October 1, 1823, for $147 (44-238).

Levi Torrey paid $160 for the land which he occupied, on October 16, 1823. Deed was witnessed by John Cook (44-239).

Ebenezer Joyce paid $130.27 for 68 acres of land on which he lives. October 3, 1823.

Abel E. Staples paid $175 for land which he occupied 1823.

James Joyce bought of Rufus B. Allyn the place on which he lived for $146.51 on May 27, 1824.

Francis T. Gilley, of Placentia, paid $237. This mortgage was paid December 25, 1839.

Robert Mitchell paid $210 for land on Placentia May 24, 1824. This mortgage was paid October 27, 1828.

Benjamin Smith bought for $365.50 the farm on which he lived, May 18, 1824.

Moses Staples' land amounted to $83.37. Recorded May 20, 1824.

Benjamin Stinson's was valued at $200.

John Staples, a lot near Mackerel Cove, for $60.75. May 17, 1824.

Benjamin F. Staples' lot valued at $42.13. Deed given May 18, 1824.

Moses Staples, jr., bought his lot for $158.16 May 17, 1824.

Daniel Hamblen, for part of Placentia, $140.30, 93 acres, 1825.

Israel B. Lunt, unincorporated place called Long island. His tract of land contained 1,132 acres, for which he was to pay $600. Date of mortgage June 30, 1835.

O'Maley at present in Paris, kingdom of France, sold to Thomas Colomey for $200 a lot near Seal Cove, executed by Rufus B. Allyn on July 1, 1835 (60-424).

Scarcely anything was paid on the above mortgages, but no action seems to have been taken by Allyn to enforce payment. Afterwards ex-Governor Edward Kent was said to have been employed by O'Maley to bring suit against the settlers to recover possession of the islands, and to have prosecuted these claims for several years. Some of the settlers paid something, as we have noticed above, while others absolutely refused to pay. In the end

Governor Kent could not find his clients and returned to the islanders what money he had collected from them. It is probable that Swan's heirs took this method to get something out of the islands, but, finding the matter likely to be hotly contested, gave up the contest.

No further claim was ever made by O'Maley or his heirs. Nothing more was done until after Col. Swan's death, when Charles J. Abbott, of Castine, was appointed administrator of the estate of James Swan, late of France, in April, 1837. Swan's just debts were $142,995.49. There not being personal property enough to pay, some of these islands were appraised by Thomas Cobb, John B. Redman and Benjamin Rea in December, 1837, as follows:

ISLAND.	ACRES.	AMOUNT.
Little Marshall	42	$63
W	10	10
A	21	21
B	4	4
C	44	66
D	16	80
F	20	30
G	33	49
K	5	6
N	23	46
P	16	16
I	6	5
John's	20	50
U	17	17
V	3	3
		$466

This took in the islands that had few or no settlers. How Mr. Abbott settled with the Swan heirs I do not know. He afterwards claimed title to some of the islands.

Up to 1834 the settlers on Swan's Island had no title to their lands except such as they could hold by possession. Neither O'Maley nor Swan ever made any claim after Mr. Abbott sold the outlying islands. We do not know what became of O'Maley. He was last heard from in Paris in 1837, where it is said that he died. A diligent search of the records of Baltimore reveals no account of him or his heirs.

In 1834 Swan's Island was organized as a plantation, when all the property was taxed. In the plantation records of 1839 we find the following land taxed to Michael O'Maley: Seven hundred acres in the southeastern part of the island, and one lot of one hundred and fifty acres bounded by the land of Benjamin Stinson and Benjamin Smith. O'Maley's tax remained unpaid, and in Hancock registry (85-33) is the following: Benjamin F. Staples, treasurer of plantation of Swan's Island, hereby certifies that real estate assessed in the year 1843 to Michael O'Maley, or unknown, on which a tax of $13.44 remains unpaid at the end of five years, said property was taken possession of by said plantation; dated July 7, 1848.

In the year 1847 John Dodge made a survey of all unappropriated lands on Swan's Island, and it was divided into lots of fifty acres each, which were numbered and divided into first, second and third class, according to their value. Some of the better lots were sold at public auction.

Many of the other lots, which were of no income to the plantation, were given to settlers. They would choose what land they wished to own, make a record of the boundaries in the book of the plantation clerk, and pay the taxes on the land so occupied. I do not know that the plantation ever gave a deed to the occupants of these lots; all of them have now become the property of private individuals.

CHAPTER III.

A SKETCH OF THE LIFE OF COL. JAMES SWAN.

James Swan was the original purchaser of the twenty-five islands included in the Burnt Coat group. The largest of these islands, which contains this town, was named for him—Swan's Island. He was born in Fifeshire, Scotland, in 1754, and came to this country about the year 1765. Although a small boy, he was unusually active and intelligent, and soon found employment in Boston. As a boy he was studious, devoting all his spare time to his books, and in this way secured an excellent education.

Even in his younger years, Swan had a varied experience. Before his twenty-second year he had been merchant, politician, soldier and author. When only eighteen years of age, while yet but a clerk in a counting-house, which was situated next to Ellis Gray's, opposite the east end of Faneuil hall, he wrote and published a work on the African slave trade. This book was published in 1772, and was entitled: "A Dissuasion of Great Britain and Her Colonies from the Slave Trade." A copy of this work is said to be in the Boston public library.

He served as an apprentice for several years with Thaxter & Son, and while there he formed an intimate friendship with several other clerks, who, in after years, became widely known. Among these were Benjamin

Thompson, afterwards made Count Rumford by the king of Bavaria; and Henry Knox, who was a clerk, probably in the same store, and afterwards became the bookseller on Cornhill, and later a general in the Continental army.

While young Swan was here employed, he boarded on Hanover street. This was at the time of the birth of the Boston Tea Party. Swan had taken a great interest in the stirring events which were transpiring just previous to the Revolutionary war, and all his sympathies were awakened in behalf of the Americans, who were manfully resisting the tyrannical laws by which Great Britain was trying to enslave the colonists.

To resist more effectually these unjust laws, an association was formed called the Sons of Liberty. Swan and the other apprentices joined the association, and he was present and took part in that act of disloyalty to the crown, which became a part of the world's history—the Boston Tea Party.

England, alarmed at the show of resistance which the colonists were making, repealed all the obnoxious laws except the tax on tea, but the colonists would not submit even to that tax. So an immense meeting was held in Faneuil hall to discuss this matter, and it was there decided that the tea in the ships then lying in Boston harbor should never be brought ashore. Accordingly, a party of the Sons of Liberty, disguised as Indians, went aboard the ships and emptied three hundred and forty-two chests of tea into the water.

History reveals that while these young men were on

their way home from the Boston Tea Party, they passed the house at which Admiral Montague, a British officer, was spending the evening. This officer raised the window and cried out:

"Well, boys, you've had a fine night for your Indian caper. But, mind, you've got to pay the fiddler yet."

"O, never mind," replied one of the leaders, "never mind, squire! Just come out here, if you please, and we'll settle the bill in two minutes."

The admiral thought best to let the bill stand, and quickly shut down the window.

When Swan and his companions returned to their boarding-place with tea in their shoes and smooched faces, they ran the gauntlet of the boarders at the next morning's breakfast. Among others who were in the Tea Party were Samuel Gore, who lived to the advanced age of ninety-eight years, George Robert, who died at the age of ninety-two, and Samuel Sprague, father of the poet.

Swan was engaged in the battle of Bunker Hill, where he was twice wounded. It is said that he was volunteer aid to Gen. Warren, but this is improbable, as all accounts of that battle show that Warren declined command, and was killed while fighting in the ranks with a musket. So it was not likely that he had an aid-de-camp.

Swan was afterwards promoted to captain in Craft's artillery. He was at the evacuation of Boston by the British on March 17, 1776. The next day he witnessed the entrance of Washington into Boston amid great rejoicing, as the inhabitants had been besieged for eleven months. Afterwards Swan became secretary of the Massachusetts board of war. He was elected a member of the legislature and adjutant-general of the state. At the close of the war he was major of a cavalry corps. Throughout the whole war, he occupied positions of trust, often requiring great courage and cool judgment, and the fidelity with which every duty was performed was shown by the honors conferred upon him after retiring to civil life.

Prior to the Revolutionary war, there was a man living in Boston named Barnaby Clark, who was a merchant and shipowner. He had two children, Samuel and Hepzibah. The latter, in 1776, became the wife of James Swan.

There was also living in Boston at this time a wealthy Scot—an old bachelor—named William Dennie, who was connected in business with Barnaby Clark, and in whose employ Samuel Clark sailed as shipmaster. A strong friendship existed between Barnaby Clark and William Dennie, and the latter, having no relatives in America, often said he would divide his property between the two children of the former. When he died, however, he left his whole estate to James Swan, being instigated thereto, it was believed, by Swan's influence.

Samuel Clark, Swan's brother-in-law, was a Revolutionary soldier, and was a major in one of the Boston regiments which took part, under Gen. Sullivan, in the Rhode Island campaign, which failed on account of a great storm that prevented the co-operation of the French troops. In this storm Major Clark contracted a disease of which he died in Boston at the age of twenty-six years, leaving a widow and infant son—also Samuel Clark. (The latter was the father of my informant, Samuel C. Clark, who now resides in Marietta, Georgia, at the advanced age of ninety years. He was a neighbor of the Swan family in Boston, and an intimate friend.)

By Major Clark's will all his property was divided between his wife and son, and he made James Swan one of the executors of the will and guardian of the child. His will gave directions as to the investments and care of the estate, none of which was observed by Colonel Swan, and when Samuel Clark became of age, twenty years after, he was only able to obtain his property by a lawsuit with Swan. Swan, by means of the large fortune willed to him, entered the mercantile business on a large scale, and became very wealthy.

At the beginning of the Revolution he was said to own about two and a half million acres of land in Mingo, Logan, Wyoming, and McDowell counties, in western Virginia; Pike county, Kentucky, and Tazewell county, Virginia. He sold what he could of this land, and devoted the proceeds to furthering the cause of American independence. In return for his services the state of Virginia redeeded to him all the property he sold, and gave him much more lying west of the Alleghanies. He also bought much of the confiscated property of the Tories. Among others was the estate belonging to Governor Hutchinson, lying on Tremont street, between West and

Boylston streets, Boston, which became very valuable property. There was also on the southerly side of Dudley street, near Dorchester, an estate of one Colonel Estes Hatch, who died, leaving it to his son Nathaniel, who was a Tory and who went to Halifax in 1776. The state confiscated the property of about sixty acres. It was purchased by Colonel Swan in 1780 for £18,000, and afterwards offered for sale to Governor Hancock for £40,000, but he would not pay the price Swan demanded.

In 1784 Swan purchased the Burnt Coat group of islands. This was about the time that his friend Gen. Henry Knox came to Maine, and purchased a large tract of land in Thomaston, where he built a large mansion and spent much of the latter years of his life. Throughout their whole lives the friendship formed in their boyhood days subsisted between Colonel Swan and General Knox, and may have induced them to have taken up their residences together in Maine.

After the war, Colonel Swan lived on the corner of West and Tremont streets. This place he afterwards sold, and it was converted into a garden theatre. He also owned a house on Dudley street, near Roxbury. The last was an old-fashioned mansion. He built in Dorchester an elegant summer residence, a part of which is standing and apparently in good condition. During Swan's short residence in Boston he gave liberal entertainments, and among others who accepted his hospitality were the Marquis de Viomenil, second under Count de Rochambeau, Admiral d' Estaing, the Marquis de Lafayette, and Gen. Henry Knox.

Later Colonel Swan became deeply involved in debt from speculations which turned out badly. In 1787 he went to Paris, and through the influence of Lafayette and other men of influence, made a fortune through government contracts by supplying their army. Here he lived through all the dark days of the French Revolution. During this period he made every effort to colonize the proscribed French nobility on his lands in America. He had induced a number to immigrate and received on board his ships a vast quantity of their furniture and belongings, but before the owners could follow their furniture on board, the relentless guillotine had caught them in its hungry jaws. The laden ships put to sea and safely arrived in Boston. One of these ships was commanded by Capt. Stephen Clough, of Wiscasset, Maine. He was an eye-witness to the execution of the French queen, which fiendish act remained indelibly impressed upon his memory. He gave to his youngest daughter the name Antoinette in memory of her.

In these cargoes sent over by Colonel Swan was a great deal of elegant furniture, beautiful pieces of tapestry, family plate, and fine paintings from royal palaces. These adorned the old Swan mansion in Dorchester. Some of these are still in the possession of his descendants, but many of them have long since been disposed of. A massive silver soup tureen was bought of the family by a gentleman in Boston. If its mate could have been procured it would readily have sold for $1,000. Comparatively useless of itself, he eventually sent it to the East Indies, where it sold for $300. At a period long subsequent its companion was disposed of in Boston. A pair of andirons of elegant and elaborate workmanship was sent here from Paris, that for a number of years enjoyed a "golden" reputation. Later they became the property of the late George Blake, and after his death they were discovered to be brass gilt.

Much of the furniture, including three or four sideboards, became the property of General Knox, who was then furnishing his mansion in Thomaston. Other articles were added to the Knox mansion by James Swan, jr., who married General Knox's youngest daughter Caroline, who was the last of the family to occupy the old mansion, which for want of care and repairs went almost to ruin over her head.

These sideboards, which came into General Knox's possession, are still retained as relics in Knox county. One of them is now in Thomaston. It came into the possession of Hon. Hezekiah Prince, of Thomaston, in 1813, when he resided in the house at Mill River, built and furnished by Knox for his son Henry. The dwelling-house and many other portions of the Knox estates had passed into the hands of his creditors. This sideboard and other furniture of Henry, jr., remained in the house and was sold, and bought by Mr. Prince. It remained in the Prince family nearly a quarter of a century. It is now owned by Charles S. Coombs, of Thomaston. Another was bought by Samuel Fuller, of Thomaston, and sold to Boston parties.

Prince Talleyrand was conveyed to Boston by Colonel Swan, and sent to Montpelier, the home of Knox in Thomaston, about 1794, where he was for some time the guest of the general.

Mrs. Swan accompanied her husband on several trips to Paris. But on his last trip Colonel Swan came to grief. He had contracted a debt in France claimed to be 2,000,000 francs. This indebtedness he denied, and refused to pay it. He was caused to be arrested by the French government and confined in St. Pelagie, a debtors' prison, from the year 1808 to 1830—a period of twenty-two years.

Swan steadfastly denied the charge brought against him, and although he was able to settle the debt, he preferred to remain a prisoner rather than secure his liberty on an unjust plea. He proposed, by a lifelong captivity if necessary, to protest against his pretended creditor's injustice. He gave up his wife, children and friends, and the comforts of his Parisian and New England homes for a principle. He made preparations for a long stay in prison.

Swan's sincere friend, Lafayette, in vain tried to prevail upon him to forego his designs of living and dying in St. Pelagie. But, no; he was stubborn to the last. He lived in a little cell in the prison, and was treated with great respect by the other prisoners, they putting aside their little furnaces with which they cooked, that he might have more room for exercise. Not a day passed without some kind act on his part, and he was known to have been the cause of the liberation of many poor debtors. When the jailer introduced his pretended creditor he would politely salute him and say to the former:

"My friend, return me to my chamber."

Here in prison for long years he remained, until, on July 28, 1830, on the ascension of Louis Philippe to the throne of France, he was forced out of prison with the other debtors at the age of seventy-six years. This St. Pelagie was the prison where Mme. Roland, of whom Thiers speaks so beautifully, and the infamous Du Barry, mistress of Louis XV, were taken to execution, and where Josephine experienced her first vicissitude of fortune, as related in the beautiful story of her life by Imbert de St. Amand.

With funds sent to him by his wife in America, Swan hired apartments in the Rue de la Clif, opposite St. Pelagie, which he caused to be fitted up at great expense, in which were dining and drawing-rooms, coaches and stables and out-houses. There he invited his friends and lodged his servants, putting at the disposal of the former his carriages in which they drove to the promenade, the ball, the theatre — everywhere in his name. At this Parisian home he gave great dinners, but as in that beautiful play of the "Lost Man" in which William Rufus Blake was so grand as Geoffrey Dale, there was always a place left for the absent one at the table. Swan seemed happy in thus braving his creditors and judges. He allowed his beard to grow, dressed *a la mode*, and was cheerful to the last day of his confinement.

When the Revolution of 1830 discharged the debtors from St. Pelagie, this brave old man (who had passed through our Revolutionary war, one of the bravest men of his day, as well as through the horrors of the French Revolution) went with them. Three days after, on July 31, he returned to St. Pelagie to reinstate himself a prisoner — for what could this old man, who had passed nearly a third of his life a prisoner, do? Here he was seized with a hemorrhage, and died suddenly in the Rue d' Echiquier, very near to where the firm of Jordan, Marsh & Co. have their foreign office.

After his freedom his one desire was to embrace his friend Lafayette, and this he did on the steps of the Hotel de Ville. The next morning Col. Swan was dead. He is said to have been a fine-looking old gentleman, greatly resembling the great philospher and statesman, Benjamin Franklin. Col. Swan's romantic career seems to have had many elements of greatness, which were especially shown by his sacrifice and heroism during the dark days of our Revolution, as well as by the many deeds of charity and liberal hospitality which characterized his whole life. It is to be regretted that his otherwise noble and generous character should have been blemished by his financial transactions.

Col. Swan had an interesting family which he left in his New England home during his long stay in Paris. His wife, Hepzibah Clark Swan, together with Hon. Jonathan Mason, who died in 1831, owned the Mt. Vernon place, which Mrs. Swan occupied during her husband's long stay in France. She was a woman of great personal beauty, of strong impulses, and a most marked and decided character. Col. Swan remitted to his wife large sums of money which were invested for her use, and were subject to her power of appointment. Besides this she received two-tenths of all the income of the Dorchester estates, and numerous other properties in Boston. Repeated attempts were made to get at his estates in Boston, as having been purchased with his creditors' funds, but they were unsuccessful. Mrs. Swan for some time lived in the elegant mansion in Boston now owned by Benjamin Wells, on Chestnut street, and also the beautiful summer residence in Dorchester. In the garden of this mansion is still to be seen the enclosure where lies buried Gen. Henry Jackson, the original trustee who had charge of her property. Mrs. Swan died in 1826. Col. and Mrs. Swan were the parents of four children—one son and three daughters, the latter of whom have many descendants in Boston, New York and Philadelphia.

Their son, James Keadie Swan, was born in 1783, and was graduated from Harvard college in 1802. He was described as "a spoiled child of wealth and dissipation, with no business, no capacity, little taste, and no means of getting a livelihood but by a yearly allowance from his mother". He married, as was said at the time, "through the influence of two scheming mothers", Caroline F., the youngest daughter of Gen. Henry Knox, of

Thomaston, in 1808. She was sixteen years of age, and a most amiable and charming person. After the marriage Swan took up his residence in Thomaston at the old Knox mansion, where his wife endured him for twenty-eight years. He died March 22, 1836, over fifty years of age.

Mrs. Swan married July 31, 1837, the Hon. John Holmes, of Alfred; this was his second marriage. He was one of the most distinguished men of his time in Maine—United States senator, United States district attorney, etc. He removed to Thomaston, repaired and occupied the Knox mansion. The second marriage of Mrs. Swan was as happy as the first had been unhappy. Mrs. Holmes died in Thomaston Oct. 17, 1851, aged sixty-one years. She left no children.

One of Mrs. Swan's daughters married John C. Howard, who died leaving several children, two of whom were married in Boston—one to Rev. Francis Wayland, D. D., late president of Brown university, and the other to Rev. C. A. Bartol, of the West church, Boston.

Another daughter married William Sullivan. She was a most refined, amiable and ladylike person, and her husband was equally distinguished; his elegant manners, kind disposition and considerate notice of the young made him very popular. His graceful and elegant hospitality and the charming society of his beautiful and accomplished family made his home delightful to all friends and visitors. One of their daughters was married to the talented artist Stewart Newton, and after his death she became the wife of Mr. O'Key, of New York. Seldom, if ever, has there gathered within the walls of one of Boston's mansions a more agreeable family.

Sullivan was a man of culture and refinement. He published an interesting volume entitled: "Familiar Letters on Public Characters." At the bar he was a pleasing speaker, and took high rank in his profession.

The third and last daughter of Mrs. Swan was married in succession to John Turner Sargent, esq., and to Rev. Dr. Richmond. After the death of the latter, she, by permission of the legislature, resumed the family name of her first husband. For several years she occupied her mother's mansion in Dorchester. In early life she was pre-eminently distinguished for beauty. Her real name was Christiana Keadie, but she was always called Kitty Swan. She was the mother of three sons, one of whom, John T. Sargent, was well known as a minister in Boston. Another had a cultivated musical taste. He published a volume of poems. He was the father of the young Kitty to whom he recently dedicated a graceful and pleasing song.

In Hancock registry is the record of the will of "James Swan, of Dorchester, U. S., now in Paris, made in prison Sept. 9, 1824, proved May 7, 1831". He names in it his wife, Hepzibah Clark, sister Margaret, widow of David Swan, of Leith, Scotland; brother David Cowper, for services in France; brother-in-law John Nixon, who is employed in the N. E. Glass Works in Boston, for loss he met in removing from Nova Scotia to Boston; oldest daughter Hepzibah Clark, widow of John Clark Howard, of Boston; Christiana Keadie, widow of John Turner Sargent, of Boston; Sally or Sarah Webb, wife of William Sullivan, and son James Keadie, "who has a bad description." Mrs. Swan and William Sullivan were named as executors. In his will he donated large sums of money to his children, and to the city of Boston to found an institution called the Swan Orphan Academy. Charles P. Ross was appointed administrator, but the estate was declared insolvent. Joseph May and William Minot were appointed commissioners, and they reported the claims against the estate to be:

Joseph Prince, judgment	$ 19,749 60
William Sullivan, trustee	28,866 01
William Sullivan	10,106 95
Jean Claude Piquet	5,841 90
Antonio Furey Piquet, administrator of the estate of Jean Claude Piquet, judgment in the circuit court	126,997 76
William Sullivan, judgment in the supreme judicial court of Massachusetts	5,473 34
	$197,055 56
Sullivan's claim disallowed	38,972 95
Amount Swan owed	$158,082 61

The estate was hopelessly insolvent, for but little property in Swan's name was found.

CHAPTER IV.

BIOGRAPHICAL SKETCHES OF EARLY SETTLERS.

Thomas Kench.

Thomas Kench was the first white settler within the present territorial limits of Swan's Island. He was an Englishman by birth, and came here near 1777, and settled on Harbor island. He built a log house and cleared a small farm, and soon bought a cow and a few sheep. Here he lived like Robinson Crusoe, many years alone, no habitation visible; the nearest settlement was at Mt. Desert. The fishing-boats passing this island, and seeing the smoke curling up above the trees from the chimney of this little isolated abode, would land to see who this lonely dweller could be. They found a reserved, eccentric man who did not encourage their visits. Many incredulous stories were told concerning him, but, no doubt, they had their origin in the minds of the imaginative fishermen.

Kench planted an oyster bed at Old Harbor, but it is not known whether it proved profitable or not. Oyster shells have been found in abundance in the soil around Mr. Kench's old cellar, which can still be seen near the shore of Old Harbor.

Kench was a Revolutionary soldier in the service of the American colonies, and was one of those who accompanied Benedict Arnold up the Kennebec river and across the wilderness to Quebec in 1775. During this march the soldiers suffered terribly from exposure and for want of food. When they arrived Arnold, in conjunction with Gen. Montgomery, with only one thousand men, besieged the city for three weeks. At last it was decided to hazard an assault. In the midst of a terrible snowstorm, they led their forces to the attack. Kench is said to have been one of the few who reached the top of the wall, but was obliged to jump down to save his life. They were soon overpowered by superior numbers, and were obliged to surrender. A remnant of the army, crouching behind mounds of snow and ice, blockaded the city until spring. At the approach of British reinforcements, they escaped and made their way homeward, disheartened by failure and sickened by want and exposure. Kench was among this small band of survivors of this most dreadful campaign of the Revolution.

Soon afterwards Kench deserted from the army, and came here, where he could be free from molestation, preferring the solitude of his island home to the horrors of warfare. No other person came to share his solitude, and he held undisputed possession of this island until after Swan's purchase, when, in 1791, David Smith brought his family to Harbor island.

In 1796 Kench removed from the place that had been his solitary abode for so many years, and went to what is now the town of Brooksville. There he bought of Edward Howard one hundred acres of land fronting on Buck's Harbor, for which he paid $100. (4-14.) He spent the remainder of his life as a farmer. He died there, over ninety years of age. His wife was Miss Jane Maker, of Cutler, whom he married soon after going to Brooksville, and by whom he had six children, three sons and three daughters. His sons Thomas and William lived and died at Brooksville. The other son, Stephen, settled in Dedham. His oldest daughter, Betsy, was the wife of a Mr. Witherspoon, who lived on Butter island in Penobscot bay. Mary was the wife of John Ross, of Brunswick. After his death she married Jephtha Benson, who lived for many years on Marshall's island. After her second husband's death she came to this island and lived with her son until her death, which occurred in 1874, at the age of eighty-two years. The last daughter, Lucy, was the wife of a Mr. White, of Orland.

David Smith.

David Smith, who was commonly called "King David", was the first permanent settler on this island. He was born in 1760, in New Hampshire, where he spent the early part of his life. He was married there and had three children. Concerning his first wife and children we have no record. When the Revolutionary war broke out, he was a lad sixteen years old. He left his home and enlisted in the New Hampshire regiment under Gen. Cilley. He served throughout the war, being in many of the engagements of the North. He fought at the battle of Bennington, Vermont, where, it will be remembered, the

Americans had collected a large amount of supplies. Burgoyne sent a detachment under Col. Baum to seize them. Gen. Stark with the militia met him there. As Stark saw the British lines forming he exclaimed:

"There are the redcoats. We must beat them to-day, or Betty Stark is a widow."

His bravery so inspired these raw troops that they defeated the British regulars, and took six hundred prisoners. Smith was also at the battle of Bemis Heights, near Saratoga, where he was badly wounded. For his services during the Revolutionary war he received a pension during the remainder of his life.

After the close of the war he came to Maine, with many others who were then leaving the older states to take up land in the district of Maine, which was then being rapidly developed. He settled at first at Deer Isle, where he lived for five years. Here, on October 23, 1786, he married Eunice, daughter of John Thurston, who came to Deer Isle in 1784 from Gloucester, Massachusetts. By this wife Smith had sixteen children. In 1791 he came here with the other workmen employed at Swan's saw and grist mills, and for a number of years he worked at the mills. He lived for a few years on Harbor Island, and afterwards moved into the "Big House". His wife died in 1809.

No longer having employment at the mills, Smith bought of Rufus B. Allyn, Swan's agent, a tract of two hundred and forty acres of land at the "North". One hundred acres of this land is now owned by his grandson,

Benjamin Smith, esq., one hundred acres by Capt. John C. Kent, and forty acres by Charles Kent. On this place he first built a log house near where Charles Kent now lives, and later built a timber house forty feet square, which was located just across the highway from Capt. John C. Kent's house.

After the death of his second wife, he married Betsey, daughter of George Gross, who came to Deer Isle in 1784 from Harpswell. Gross was a Revolutionary soldier, and was pensioned by the government. By this wife Smith had eight children—twenty-four in all after coming here, besides the three by his first wife in New Hampshire. Mrs. Smith died in 1868, aged eighty years.

After moving upon this tract of land Smith cleared a fine farm, and spent the remainder of his life as a successful farmer. The soil was then rich, and excellent crops were harvested. He died in 1840, aged eighty years. Most of his large and interesting family settled here. Their children were as follows:

John, born in 1787, was lost at sea while engaged in the West India trade, at about the age of twenty-one years.

Eunice, who was born in 1789, became the wife of Anthony Merchant, jr., of Merchant's island. He was born in 1790. Merchant's father settled Merchant's island, and from him it received its name. They had one son, David S., and one daughter, who became the wife of Willard Mathews, who at that time resided on Merchant's island. After his marriage he removed to

Belfast out of which place he sailed for a number of years as master mariner. After Eunice's death, Mr. Merchant married Maria Gross. He was for many years collector of taxes in the Isle au Haut collection district, and was a faithful and efficient officer. He died about 1865, at the age of seventy-five years.

David, 2d, born in 1791. These three children were born at Deer Isle previous to his coming here.

Sarah, born in 1792, on Harbor island, became the wife of Benjamin Stinson, esq.

Benjamin, born in 1795, at the "Big House". He was the first white child born on this island.

George, born in 1799, never married.

Asa was born in 1803.

Ann, wife of Benjamin Kent, was born in 1808.

All the rest of the children by his second wife died in childhood.

By his third wife his children were: John; Mary, who became the wife of Samuel Kent; Eliza, wife of Johnson Billings; James; Lucy, wife of John Stinson, who after his death married John Valentine and lived at Irish point; William; Dorothy, who married Benjamin Smith, 2d; Solomon, who died young.

Smith's sons, named above, being among the young settlers, most of whom were the first settlers on the land they occupied, will be further noticed.

I. *David Smith*, *2d*, took up a tract of one hundred acres of land, a part of which is now occupied by Pearl Smith, and built a house near where he now lives. This land was a part of the property which had been taxed to O'Maley, but failing to pay the tax thereon for many years, the plantation took possession of it, after which it was taken up by settlers. In 1840 Mr. Smith married Lucy Gross, daughter of George Gross, before mentioned, by whom he had eleven children. Mr. Smith died in 1868, aged seventy-seven years. His wife died in 1886, aged eighty-seven years. The following were their children:

Betsey, wife of Edmond Stanley; Abigail, wife of Joseph Stanley; Susan, who was three times married, her first husband being Joseph Dunbar, from whom she was separated; her second husband was Joseph Smith, of Jonesport; her third, Peter Stanley; David, 3d; Asa, who died at sea; Mary A., wife of Moses Conary; Lois, wife of Samuel Whitmore, of Deer Isle; Sarah J., who married Curtis Robinson and now resides in Boston; Dorinda, who died unmarried; George W.; Lucy, wife of Charles Little, of Rockland.

II. *Benjamin Smith* took up the tract of land adjoining his father's on the south which extended to the Stewart lot. It contained one hundred and thirty-six acres, and was bought of Swan and O'Maley's agent. He afterwards took up a lot of fifty acres of the proprietors' lots, such as were mentioned in the last sketch. This adjoined the land of his brother David. He built a house on the hill near where the Irish point road joins the highway.

Mr. Smith was an enterprising, intelligent man, taking an interest in all public affairs. He served on the first board of assessors after the plantation was organized in 1834. His other associates on the board were Benjamin Stinson and James Joyce. He was a firm friend of the public schools, doing much to encourage their establishment. He offered the use of his house in which the first term of public school was taught on this island. The next year a schoolhouse was built. Previous to this time all schools had been supported by private donations.

Mr. Smith's wife was Marjory, daughter of Elijah Toothaker, who came to Deer Isle in 1798 from Phillips, in Franklin county. He was drowned near 1810; while coming from the main land he accidentally fell overboard. Mrs. Toothaker was married five times. After Mr. Toothaker's death she married in succession, Belcher Tyler. Thomas Stinson, 2d, Samuel Jordan and Dominicus Carman. Mr. Smith died in 1872, aged seventy-seven years. His wife died in 1882, aged eighty-eight years.

Mrs. Smith was the mother of ten children—six sons and four daughters. The daughters were: Eunice, wife of Moses B. Sadler; she died in Rockland in 1863, aged forty-three years; Phebe, widow of David E. Sprague; Betsey, wife of David Smith, 3d; she died in 1891, at the age of fifty-nine years; Lucinda, who died from the effects of scalding. The sons were: Elijah, who died of yellow fever while on a voyage from Wilmington to Guadeloupe; he was mate with Capt. Thomas Bunker, of Cranberry Isles; Sylvanus, who died young; Benjamin, 2d, who occupies a part of the lot taken up by his grandfather, David Smith, sr., and who has been one of the foremost men of the town, holding every town office in the gift of the people; he possessed a wonderful memory; he was well read in ancient and modern history, and he possessed the faculty, that so few people have, of remembering exactly names and dates; it was from him I received much information concerning the early settlers and their family histories; Newell, who died in Rio Janeiro while there in command of a vessel; his home was in Rockland; he married Clara Sadler, who now resides in Somerville; Eben, who was lost at sea on a voyage from New York to Havana, as mate of a schooner; she had a deck-load of shooks; as he was coming on deck during a severe gale, a sea swept the deck-load overboard, carrying him with it; his first wife was Betsey Brown, of Vinalhaven, from whom he was divorced; they had one child, who is now the widow of Hiram Colomy; he afterwards married Mary Sadler; after Mr. Smith's death she became the wife of David H. Sprague; Andrew, who married Clementine Lancester; while preparing for college he studied under Rev. Jonathan Adams; he was graduated from Bowdoin college, and later attended the theological seminary at Bangor, and became a Congregational minister; he preached at Camden, Boothbay and Waterford; at the latter place he died.

 III. *Asa Smith* settled at first near Irish point, where he built a log house. He changed his residence several times. He lived at Mount Desert; afterwards he came back here, and lived where Hezekiah Holbrook now resides; later he went to Deer Isle, and finally to

Saco, where he died. His wife was Abigail Kent, by whom he had ten children — six sons and four daughters.

The daughters were: Elmira, who became the wife of Benjamin Gould, of Rockland; she separated from him and afterwards married in Boston; Catherine, who married Solomon Morgan, of New York; Melissa, who married Charles Holmes, of Boston, an excellent man, in easy circumstances; it was with Mr. Holmes that his wife's father spent his declining years; after Mr. Holmes died his widow married again and resides in Saco; Asenath, who also married in Saco.

The sons were: Samuel, who moved to Jonesport and married Julia Alley, of that place; he possessed a shiftless character; he left his wife and went to Grand Menan, where he died; Asa, 2d, who married Jane E. Davis, of Long Island, from whom he was divorced; while here he lived in the Billings house just north of where Capt. John C. Kent now lives; later he married, in 1858, Abbie Hunt, of Rockland; Henry, who, when about twenty years of age, left home for "life on the ocean wave"; for a long time he was not heard from, but he was seen in New York city by an acquaintance from this island; he was in a large ship about to start for China; since then he has never been heard from; George, who was drowned in the cove near Buckle island; his brother Alden was in bathing, and having got beyond his depth, was in imminent danger of drowning; George went to his rescue, but became exhausted and sank, and before assistance came he was dead; Alden and Eldad, both of whom left town, and their whereabouts is unknown.

IV. *John Smith* bought the lot known as the Irish point farm of Samuel Kent. This place is now owned by the heirs of Capt. John Staples and David Smith, 3d. Mr. Smith married Lydia Rich, of Mount Desert. He died in 1876, at the age of sixty-five years. His wife died five years before, aged sixty years. They were the parents of six children — two sons, Benjamin and Frank, who died young, and four daughters. The oldest daughter, Angeline, married Hezekiah Holbrook; Athalana was the wife of William Withrow, of Nova Scotia; Lenora, now dead, was the wife of Warren Smith. One other daughter, Margaret, died young.

V. *James Smith* took up the lot north of his father, David Smith, sr. This is known as the "Narrows lot"; it includes the northern extremity of the island. The place is now owned by J. T. Crippen, of Ellsworth. On this place are located some valuable stone quarries. Mr. Smith married Mary Stewart, by whom he had four children—the present Leroy and Albion Smith, and two daughters—Matilda, wife of Moses Sadler, and Edna, who died young.

VI. *William Smith*, the last son of David Smith, sr., married Prudence Gott. He built the house where Capt. John C. Kent now lives. Afterwards he went to Deer Isle, where he bought a farm near Stinson's Neck bar. He died in 1890, aged sixty-eight years. His widow resides at Stonington.

Joseph Toothaker.

Joseph Toothaker came here a short time after Mr. Smith, probably the same year, from Phillips, in Franklin county. He settled on a lot of land north of the carrying-place. He built a house whose location can still be seen near the cove just across the carrying-place. On April 26, 1792, Joseph Prince gave him a bond of $100 for a deed of one hundred acres of land beginning at the carrying-place and extending around the cove far enough to include one hundred acres, after he had occupied it seven years (3-208). If he had any family here, I do not know what became of them. He was an uncle of Benjamin Smith's wife and a brother of Elijah Toothaker, who came to Deer Isle in 1798.

Mr. Toothaker had been absent from home some time when search was made, and he was found on Harbor island, dead from the effects of a gunshot wound—whether accidental or otherwise was never known, but many suspicious circumstances led to the belief that he had been foully dealt with. The cove bordering on the carrying-place near where he lived is still called after him Toothaker's cove.

Joshua Grindle.

Joshua Grindle came here from Sedgwick in 1794. We find he sold the same year the lot he had formerly lived on "to James Douglass a lot of land at Buck's Harbor, township number 4, county of Lincoln, Massachusetts Bay, New England, for the sum of £12, s10, Hallifax currency". (3-105) He took up a tract of land here extending from Moses Staples' to the carrying-place, which contained one hundred acres. It is the lot occupied by Horace E. Stanley, Daniel McKay and others. The hill above the carrying-place is still called "Grindle hill". Joseph Prince gave a bond for a deed to Mr. Grindle on May 1, 1794, to be given when he had lived on the place for seven years.

The island having been sold to Swan again, he gave to Prince the power of attorney, Feb. 28, 1798, to give Grindle a deed, and although Grindle lived on this lot until 1800, no deed to him was ever recorded. In the year 1800 he returned to township No. 4 (Brooksville), where he bought two lots of land of Abner Dodge, where he lived on his farm the remainder of his life. He died about the year 1849, aged near seventy-five years. Mr. Grindle's wife was Ruth Stanley, of Sedgwick, whom he married before coming here, and by whom he had ten children. When he left this island his place was taken by John Van Namberg, a Dutchman, whose wife's name was Sarah. They had no children. After a short residence here, he left and went to Brooksville. Samuel Kempton afterwards took this same place. His wife was Lydia Dunham. They had one daughter, Hannah, who moved to Hampden. The property fell into the hands of Edward Gott, whose heirs still own it. Whether Mr. Grindle ever secured any title to this land or not we never learned, nor is there any record of his deeding it to the subsequent occupants.

Mr. Grindle's family consisted of four daughters and six sons. The daughters were: Anna, who became the wife of Richard Grindle and settled in Brooksville; Joanna, who was the wife of Israel Johnson, and resided in Bluehill; Mary, who married William Wescott, and lived at North Bluehill; Eliza, who died young.

The sons were: Eben, who was born here in 1800; his wife was Mary Grindle; he was the father of Mrs. E. J. Orcutt, whose husband was formerly light-keeper at Hocomock Head; Stephen, whose wife was Hulda Snow; their home was in Brooksville; Lowell, who married Mary Stephenson and lived in Surry for many years, finally returning to Brooksville where they died; Joshua, who married Mercy Farnham and settled in Surry; John, who married Eliza Smith and settled in Surry; Daniel, who married Ruth Rogers and settled in Salem, Mass.

All the children of Mr. Grindle, sr., survived him except Eliza. They are now all dead except Joshua.

Alexander Nutter.

Alexander Nutter was the first settler on Irish point. He came here about 1796 from Gloucester, Mass. He first came to the island in a coasting vessel. This was after the mills were erected and the manufacture of lumber was begun. He thought it would be an excellent opening where he could find lucrative employment coasting. So he bought a vessel and moved to this place. His wife was Betsy Kent, whom he married before coming here. He moved from this place to Mount Desert and later to Ripley's Neck in the town of Harrington, then to Gouldsboro where he took up a farm and spent the remainder of his life. He died at the age of ninety-six years. His wife died at the age of sixty-four years. They had a family of five children, of whom Amelia was the oldest. She married a Mr. Robbins, of Harrington. She died at the age of nearly ninety years. Another daughter, Salome, was twice married. Her first husband was a Mr. Wheeler. After his death she became the wife of Frederick Burns. Jonathan Nutter, the oldest son, married Louisa Cole, of Harrington, by whom he had fourteen children. One of these children, Albert, perished on the south side of Nantucket Island during a winter gale. He was mate of the schooner "Haines". They were driven ashore and the whole crew lost. Other vessels were wrecked here at the same time, and among the dead that washed ashore his body could not be recognized. Isabell was the fourth child. She married a Mr. Mitchell and resided in Boston. Reuben Nutter, the youngest child, married Ruth Frye, of Harrington. He is now an inmate of the Sailor's home, Staten Island. He is a very old man.

John Rich.

John Rich came here in 1794, and took up the first lot of land on the eastern side of the island, a part of which is now owned by Francis Torrey. He built a log house near the shore. He remained here, however, only three years, when he removed to Isle au Haut. Here he took up a lot of land north of Robert Douglass, whose daughter he married.

When Mr. Rich left here his property came into the possession of Moses Staples. It was said that he came to this place from Mt. Desert. He had many relatives there.

Mrs. Rich was a woman of prepossessing appearance. She was the mother of Capt. Stephen Rich, who removed to Gloucester, out of which place he sailed as master in the fishing business several years. He was an active, enterprising man. He was lost at sea, together with all his crew, in 1841.

Another son was Jonathan Rich, who was an invalid for many years, and died not far from the year 1864.

Another son was Thomas Rich, who was drowned in 1839.

The two remaining sons were Perez Rich, who removed to Islesboro, and Stillman Rich, who became the occupant of the property of Mr. Douglass.

There was one daughter in the family, who was the first wife of Josiah Pierce, of Vinalhaven, and they became converts to Mormonism and moved to Narvoo, Illinois. While there she became disgusted with it, and made her escape. With but little means she returned to her friends, and was divorced. She afterwards became the wife of Noah Barter. She was the mother of one daughter, who died some years ago. Mr. Rich, sr., died near the year 1860, his wife surviving him a few years.

William Davis.

William Davis, a relative of Mr. Rich, came here also in 1794. He took up the lot of land adjoining Rich on the north, now owned by Gilman Staples. He left with Rich in 1797, and went to Long Island, which furnished a better harbor to shelter his boat, and was more convenient to pursue the fishing business. Mr. Davis has many descendants at Long Island.

Richard Carpenter.

Richard Carpenter came here from some town on the Penobscot river, and took up the lot now owned by Mrs. Lenora Wharton and George E. Stanley. It contained one hundred acres. I do not know the date of his coming, but he was the first occupant of this land. His wife was Betsey Hamblen, of Gott's island, by whom he had eight children, as follows: Abigail, Nathaniel, Ambrose, Susan, Emmeline, John, Philip and Margaret. None of these children settled here. Mr. Carpenter built a house near the shore, below where Mrs. Wharton now lives, where all his children were born. He was found dead in the woods where he had gone to chop. After his death his widow sold the place and went to Bucksport, where she became the wife of Ephraim Emerson. After his death she married Charles Wheeler, of Carmel.

Moses Staples.

Moses Staples came here in 1793 from Deer Isle. He was, next to David Smith, the oldest permanent settler,

coming some two years later than Mr. Smith. He took
up a tract of one hundred acres adjoining Joshua Grindle
on the south. He was at this time the only settler on the
west side of the harbor. Here near the shore he built a
log house and brought his family. The crevices between
the logs were plastered with lime made by burning clam
shells, which were found in great quantities near where
his house stood. Its location was near where David
Smith, 3d, now lives. Mr. Staples was a ship carpenter,
and came here because building material was plenty and
cheap. Excellent ship timber was made of the trees that
grew close to the water's edge, and small vessels were
then in great demand in the coasting trade.

After living on this lot for a few years, he, in 1797,
moved to the eastern part of the island, and bought the
lots just being vacated by John Rich and William Davis.
He also took up all the land north of the Davis lot to the
salt water. So his tract of land extended from where
James Joyce now lives to the end of Trask's point. He
received a deed of this lot together with the lot near Old
Harbor from Rufus B. Allyn, Swan's agent, in 1824, in
consideration of the small sum of $83.37, and gave Allyn
a mortgage. He at first built a log house just to the eastward of Joseph W. Staples' present residence. Afterwards he built a frame house and barn. He did an
extensive business in shipbuilding at the place where
Henry D. Joyce now has his boat-shop, and it is still
called "The Yard". One of the vessels built there, the
"Arcadie", was seen in Boston nearly sixty years after

she was built, having, of course, been several times repaired.

Moses Staples was born in 1753, and in the year 1764 he came to Deer Isle with his parents. He had a younger brother named Joshua, and one older brother. He had several sisters, one of whom was Hannah, wife of Stephen Babbidge; another was the wife of Courtney Babbidge, sr., after whose death she became the wife of James Joyce, whom we shall notice as one of the early settlers here. Another sister was the second wife of Thomas Conary. By each of his wives Mr. Conary had ten sons — twenty in all. Another sister was the wife of Jonathan Torrey, and the last sister, Ann, was the wife of Timothy Saunders.

The brother Joshua spoken of married a daughter of John Raynes, sr., by whom he had one daughter, Jane, who married Elias Morey, jr., who lived and died on this island.

The father of this Staples family was impressed on board of an English man-of-war during the Revolution, and was never heard from. The mother of this family, Mrs. Mercy Staples, afterwards married a Mr. Hutchinson, of Sedgwick, by whom she had two sons and one daughter. The sons were Rev. David Hutchinson, a presiding elder in the Methodist Episcopal church in the western part of the State, and Timothy Hutchinson, who lived and died on Little Deer Isle. The daughter, Susan, was the wife of Capt. Benjamin Gray, of Penobscot.

Moses Staples married Judith Eaton, of Deer Isle,

before coming here. They were the parents of thirteen children. Their descendants formed the largest family on the island.

After Mr. Staples' marriage he went from Deer Isle to live in Sedgwick, where he remained about a year. While there their first child was born. He came back to Deer Isle. Seven children were born to them there, and after coming back to Swan's Island the remaining five were born. Mr. Staples was an active, intelligent man, who always took a great interest in the transaction of town business, and was ever foremost for public improvement.

In 1844, some two years previous to his death, he very thoughtfully had a sworn statement drawn by Joshua Trask, esq., of the dates when many of the earliest settlers came, and the lots of land taken up by them. This was prompted, no doubt, by the fact that no public records had been made. This document has been a great help in making a record of his family. He accumulated considerable property which he disposed of before his death.

The lot of land bought of John Rich, being the property of Francis Torrey and Asa Joyce, went to his son, Moses Staples, 2d, in the year 1800. The lot he bought of William Davis, which is now owned by Gilman Staples, he sold to his son-in-law, John Finney, in 1803. The place now owned by Joseph W. Staples went to his son, Abel E. Staples. The remainder of the point of land he divided into two parts; the eastern half he gave to his son Alexander, and the western half to his son Mark.

Moses Staples died in 1846 at the age of ninety-three years. His wife died three years before at the age of eighty-seven years. The children of Moses and Judith Staples were as follows:

The daughters were Elizabeth, wife of John Finney; Dorcas, wife of John Skinner; they lived and died in Boston; Mrs. Skinner died in 1839. Another daughter, Sarah, married Capt. Thomas Bunker, of Cranberry Island. He was a master mariner, and went on foreign voyages. Mrs. Bunker died at the age of forty-five years. Her children were Thomas, Marietta, Martha, Hulda, Joseph, Warren and Moses. Another daughter, Hannah, died at the age of sixteen years, and the last daughter, Judith, was the wife of Robert Mitchell.

The sons were Joshua, Alexander, Moses, Samuel, Mark, Abel, Washington and Amos. The sons and their families all settled here, and so will be further noticed.

I. *Joshua Staples* took up a lot of land adjoining his father on the west in 1819. It is the land now owned by Capt. John S. Staples. He built a house over a cellar near where Emery Barbour's house now stands. His wife was a daughter of Josiah Closson, of Deer Isle, by whom he had fourteen children. Mr. Staples moved to Sedgwick, where he died in 1860, at the age of seventy-seven years. His wife survived him several years, dying at the age of eighty-one years. The following are their children:

Abel, who, when a young man went to sea, and was gone from home eighteen years, during which time he visited nearly all parts of the world; he then came home and married Caroline Kane, of Brooklin, where he resided until his death, which took place by the capsizing of a boat in Eggmoggin Reach; although he was an excellent swimmer, he was drowned; this was due to his grasping a rope to which an anchor was attached, and which he held firmly, thus keeping his head below water until life was extinct; the other men, except John Ross, who was also drowned, saved their lives by clinging to the boat; Nathan, who settled in Sedgwick; he was a carpenter by trade; his wife was Sally Grant; Isaac, who died at the age of eighteen years; William, who lived and died at Bluehill; his wife was Irena McFarland; Ephraim, who married Caroline Merchant, of Merchant's Island, where he resided for a number of years, after which he moved to Rockland where he died: Johnson, who at present lives in Rockland; he is a carpenter by trade, and is now foreman of the South End railway; his wife was Lucy Chatto, of Long Island, in the town of Bluehill; Levi, who married Hannahetta Staples, built a house near where Joseph Remick, whom we shall notice, once settled; Capt. Ebenezer M., who lived for some time at Deer Isle, married a daughter of Alexander Staples, widow of Washington Staples — a singular occurrence, her maiden name being Staples, as well as that of her two husbands.

The daughters were: Charlotta, wife of Jonathan Bridges, of Sedgwick; Lucy, who died young; Sarah, who married first David Whipple, and after his death became the wife of John Murch, of Trenton, who is now dead; Lois, who was the wife of Levi Closson; after his death she married Pickering Eaton, of Sedgwick; she is now dead; Caroline, who was the wife of John Hamilton, of Bluehill; Lydia, who died when a child.

II. *Alexander Staples* did not occupy the land left him by his father, but sold it to Solomon Barbour, who moved here in 1843. Mr. Staples married Margaret, daughter of John Stinson, of Deer Isle. After his death she married Joseph Small, of Deer Isle. After Mr. Small's death she came here to reside. She died in 1882. Mr. and Mrs. Alexander Staples were the parents of the following children: Isabel, first wife of Asa Joyce; Elizabeth, first the wife of Washington Staples, and after his death the wife of Capt. Ebenezer Staples; Hulda, wife of William Bunker, of Cranberry Island, and who now resides in Massachusetts; Julia, wife of Benjamin Gray, and Margaret, second wife of Joseph C. Judkins. The last two reside at Deer Isle; one son, Amos, died when a child.

III. *Moses Staples*, 2d, in 1800 bought the tract of land first taken up by John Rich, extending from the Finney to the Joyce lot. His wife was Betsey Rufnelle, of Tremont, whose father was a Frenchman and came to Mount Desert from Boston. They occupied for several years a log house left by Mr. Rich, their first child being born there. He afterwards built a house that was located just across the road from where Francis Torrey now lives. Mr. Staples died in 1862, aged eighty-four years. Betsey, his wife, died in 1858, aged seventy-seven years. They were the parents of ten children, the first of whom was born in 1800. Most of the children settled here, and they were an enterprising family.

Their daughters were: Mary, wife of William Joyce; Hannah, wife of Rev. Benjamin F. Stinson; Sally, first wife of Jacob Reed, who died in 1865, aged fifty-nine years; Susan, wife of Edward Gott, who died in 1894, aged seventy-seven years. Mrs. Stinson died in 1895, aged eighty-five years. She was the last survivor of the family.

Their sons were: Franklin B., who bought the land we have spoken of as being taken up by Joshua Staples; it included all the land now owned by Capt. John S. Staples, besides the lots owned by Capt. Ebenezer M. Staples, Thomas Pinkham, Capt. Emery E. Joyce, Emery Barbour, Ellis R. Joyce and William H. Burns; his wife was Lucy R. Smith, by whom he had five children, as follows: Capt. Hezekiah Staples, who married Abigail York, of Ellsworth, where he now resides; Gilman, whose wife was Mercy Stockbridge, and resides on the Finney place; Reuben, who died young; Capt. John S., whose first wife was Rosilla Staples, who, together with her child, died of diphtheria; he afterwards married her sister, Lucy J. Staples; he owns the homestead lot; one daughter was the wife of Levi Staples; Mr. Staples died in 1879, aged seventy-eight years; Lucy R., his wife, died the same year, aged seventy-three.

Augustus R., who bought the Carpenter lot, which contained one hundred acres, of the widow of Richard

Carpenter; he built the house where George E. Stanley now lives, it being one of the oldest houses in town; his wife was Susan Hamblen, of Gott's Island; Mr. Staples was a man endowed with a good share of common sense, and was a practical business man, serving the plantation in its early days in many positions of trust; his death, which was much lamented, occurred in 1856, at the age of forty-four years; his wife died July 4, 1875, at the age of sixty-four years. Their children were: Amanda, widow of Oliver L. Joyce, esq.; Nancy, widow of Lephen Babbidge, who now resides in the West; Isadore, wife of Joseph Reed; soon after their marriage she accompanied her husband on a voyage to New York in a vessel which was lost, probably foundering in the gale which overtook them soon after leaving New York; this was in the year 1867; Mr. Reed's age was twenty-five and his wife's twenty-two years; Ida, who married Frank Staples and lives in Rockland. There were two sons, between whom their father's land was divided; Benjamin S. built a house to the eastward of his father's; his wife was Lenora Joyce; he died in 1884, at the age of forty-five years; after his death his widow married William Wharton. The other son, Augustus W., married Abbie Barbour, of Deer Isle, and resides here.

Moses, 3d, bought the Finney place and built the house standing thereon: his wife was Mercy Smith. Mr. Staples was subject to epileptic fits, and during one of these seizures he fell upon a fire and received injuries from which he died in 1845, at the age of twenty-six years.

Mrs. Staples afterward became the wife of Benjamin S. Dolliver, of Mount Desert.

Washington had a part of his father's land, being that now owned by Asa Joyce's heirs, and built the house thereon. He died in 1849, and, as has already been stated, his widow, Elizabeth, married Capt. Ebenezer M. Staples.

Simeon took his father's place, and with him his parents lived during their latter days. His wife was Saphrona Joyce. He was a carpenter, having learned his trade with John Adams. He moved from this place to Rockland. His place became the property of Francis M. Torrey. Mr. Staples died in Rockland in 1892; his widow still resides there.

IV. *Capt. Samuel Staples* married Ruth Bunker, of Cranberry Island, at which place he lived for several years, afterwards going to Lubec and finally to Bangor, where he died in 1853, aged sixty-six years. They were the parents of seven children: Hannah, Philo, Samuel, Isaac, George, Priscilla, Judith.

V. *Mark Staples* married Lydia Gott, of Mount Desert. He built a house near where John Stockbridge afterwards lived. He then sold this place and occupied the land left him by his father, which we have spoken of, it being the land now occupied by Capt. Olando Trask, Henry D. Joyce, Jefferson Torrey and Elmer I. Joyce estate. He built a house near where Capt. Trask's now stands. He afterwards moved to Aroostook county, and subsequently moved many times, being of a roving nature.

He died at Rockland in 1851, at the age of sixty-one years.

VI. *Abel E. Staples* took up the lot of land extending westward from his brother Joshua. It begins to the western line of Capt. John S. Staples' land, and extends around the cove to the land now owned by Reuben Joyce; it contained one hundred acres. He was the first settler on this land. He built a house near where Herbert W. Joyce's store now stands. In 1837 he moved upon his father's place, and lived with his parents until their death. His wife was Rebecca Whitmore, of Deer Isle. They were the parents of ten children. The daughters were: Mary E., wife of Joshua Trask, esq., who was lost in the Bay of Chaleur in the great gale of October 3, 1851, aged forty-four years; after his death she married Philip Moore, of Gott's Island; she is now dead; Abigail, wife of Stephen B. Lane, of Deer Isle; Joanna, wife of Capt. Levi Torrey; she died in 1887 at the age of sixty-six years; Harriet N., widow of Solomon Barbour; Louisa, wife of Henry D. Joyce. The sons were: Samuel W., John, Joseph, who died young, Seth W., and Joseph W.

Abel Staples died in 1851, aged sixty-six years; his wife died in 1873, aged eighty-one years. Previous to his death he divided his property among his three sons. Joseph W. and Samuel W. received the homestead lot and the western part of the lot he first took up (that lot extending from Reuben Joyce's to near the steamboat road). The rest of this lot, extending from the steamboat road to the land of Capt. John S. Staples, went to the other brother, John. Samuel died in 1883, aged sixty-two years. After his death his part of the property went to his brother Joseph W. Joseph W. married Caroline Stinson, of Deer Isle; she died in 1874, aged forty-five years; after her death he married Mrs. Ellen Stanley, of Gouldsboro. John built the house now owned by Alfred W. Joyce; he was a master mariner, and accumulated considerable property; during the latter part of his life he was engaged in trading. He was three times married; in 1841 he married Maria Barbour, who died in 1874, aged fifty-one years; after her death he married Mrs. Helen Merrill, who died in 1880, aged forty-eight years; his last wife was her sister, Mrs. Henrietta Marshall; all of his wives belonged in Deer Isle. He died in 1891, aged seventy-one years. His children were: Capt. Benjamin J., who is a merchant here; Capt. Charles, who died in 1888, aged thirty-eight years; Matilda, wife of Levi B. Joyce; Rosilla and Lucy J., wives of Capt. John S. Staples; Durilla, wife of Herbert W. Joyce; Maria, wife of Andrew Torrey. There were several other children who died young.

VII. *Washington* died when a young man. He was taken ill while on a sea voyage, and was brought into Cranberry Island, where he died.

VIII. *Amos* died young in 1807.

Joseph Remick.

Joseph Remick came here from Hancock soon after the war of 1812. For a few years he lived in a house with Deacon James Joyce; afterwards he built a house to the west of where Mrs. Hannahetta Staples now lives, the cellar of which can still be seen. Mr. Remick married Miss Priscilla Noble, of Mount Desert, by whom he had nine children. They left this place in 1830 and returned to Hancock. Later they moved to Roxbury, Mass., where Mr. Remick died in the year 1834, aged nearly fifty years. Mrs. Remick, after the death of her husband, made her home in Ellsworth, where she died. Their children were as follows: Reuben died in Ellsworth; his wife was Mary A. Finney; Nathan was lost at sea; he was with his brother returning home from a coasting trip. One day during the voyage he was at work in the yawl boat at the davits, when one of the falls broke and precipitated him into the water. He seized two oars as he fell, which kept him afloat. In the excitment of lowering the boat, the painter was dropped and the boat drifted away. The wind died away so that the vessel could not be managed. Hatches and everything that would float were thrown to the now helpless man, but being unable to swim he could not reach them. For over half an hour he sustained himself within speaking distance of the vessel. At last a small wave rolled over his head when he sank from view. He was twenty-one years of age, and was to have been married on his return home. The other children of Mr. and Mrs. Remick were Philip, who married Maria Milliken and settled in Ellsworth; Capt. Lewis Remick, who married Elizabeth Milliken; after her death he married Henrietta Jordan; they lived at Bayside, Ellsworth; Hannah was the wife of Mr. Carlton, of Boston; Catherine was the wife of George Lorn, of Boston: Phebe married Dr. John F. W. Lane, of Boston; Judith was the wife of Capt. Watts, of Ellsworth, and Margaret was the wife of Gardiner Milliken, of Ellsworth.

The only survivors of this family are Philip, Lewis and Mrs. Lane.

James Joyce.

James Joyce took up the lot adjoining Moses Staples on the south, which contained one hundred acres of land. Mr. Joyce came to Deer Isle from Marshfield, Mass., and there took up a tract of land north of Capt. Peter Hardy's, which is owned by John Thompson. It is still known as the Joyce lot. The Joyces came to America from Gloucestershire, England, or near by, where many of that name still reside. Among the members of the Joyce family there seemed to be a talent for drawing and painting. Some were quite noted artists. In the British museum there are several colored drawings of the Prophets by the Rev. James Joyce, of Fairfield church, Gloucestershire.

The earliest record of this family in America is at Marshfield, Mass., where most of their descendants still reside. There was a clock-maker there who had three sons, one of whom went to New Haven, Conn., one to Deer Isle, and one, whose name I could not learn, to some point near Lewiston or Brunswick.

When James Joyce came to Maine he settled first at a place called Majorbagwaduce near where the town of

Brooksville is now located, where he took up a tract of land which, however, he sold when he went to Deer Isle. I find the following record in Hancock registry (3-97): James Joyce of a place called Majorbagwaduce, in consideration of the sum of £50, Halifax currency, sold to Kenicum Limburner, of the same place, one hundred and fifty acres of land located on the east side of Majorbagwaduce river. This was dated October 1, 1782.

Joyce came to Swan's Island in 1806, and moved his family into the house just vacated by Joseph Prince. From here they moved into the "Big House", which at that time furnished accommodations for thirteen families. Swan's agent offered Mr. Joyce the gift of two hundred acres of land on the eastern side of the island if he would move there and build a sawmill over the stream where a gristmill was afterwards erected. He also offered him a share of the lumber so manufactured. But Mr. Joyce did not accept the offer.

In a few years, however, he moved to the eastern side, and took up the land I have mentioned. He cut away the immense growth of pine trees, cleared the land for cultivation, and built a log house near where the Reed house now stands. He afterwards built a house to the eastward of where James Joyce, 3d, now lives, where he spent the remainder of his life, the latter years of which he lived with his son William.

Joyce's wife was Mary Staples, a sister of Moses Staples, sr., and at this time was the widow of Courtney Babbidge, sr. Mr. and Mrs. Joyce were the parents of eight children, three sons — James, Ebenezer and William, and five daughters — Elethea, wife of Jeremiah Weed: Mercy, wife of Courtney Babbidge; Olive, wife of Capt. Levi Torrey; Abigail, wife of Samuel Whitmore, and Ruth, wife of John Stockbridge. Of these daughters, Mrs. Weed and Mrs. Whitmore remained on Deer Isle, and Mrs. Babbidge died in Ellsworth.

Mr. Joyce's descendants form a large and influential family, most of whom remained here. They have always been prominent in educational matters, and they have been represented among the officers of this place almost every year since the plantation was organized. Mr. Joyce died in 1833, aged seventy-five years. His wife died in 1836, at the age of seventy-five years. The sons, all of whom settled here, will be further noticed.

Deacon James Joyce, the oldest son of James Joyce, sr., in 1816 took up a tract of one hundred acres adjoining his father on the south. He built a log house to the eastward of where Levi B. Joyce's house now stands. He afterwards built a house of hewn timber, and later built the house that Levi B. Joyce now owns. His property is in part owned by his two sons, Levi B. and Oliver L.

Mr. Joyce was the first deacon of the Baptist church after its organization here. He died in 1873, aged seventy-nine years. His wife died in 1872, aged seventy-two years. His wife was Jane, a daughter of John Stinson, of Deer Isle, by whom he had twelve children — seven daughters and five sons. The daughters were: Mary, wife of Levi Babbidge, who resided in Rockland; Isabel S., third wife of Jacob S. Reed; she died in 1888, at the age of sixty-eight years; Jane, wife of William A. Friend, of Sedgwick; she is now dead; Abigail, wife of Isaac H. Marks, of Sedgwick; they afterward moved to Rockland, where Mr. Marks died; his widow still resides there; Margaret, wife of William Pickering, of Deer Isle; Nancy, wife of Rodney Gott, who now resides in Somerville, Mass., and Sarah, wife of James H. Hutchingson, of Mansfield.

All five of the sons settled in this town, and were as follows: Asa, who married Isabel Staples, of Deer Isle, at which place he resided for some years; he then came to this island and built the house now owned by Warren Sprague; after the death of Washington Staples, he bought that farm, on which he has ever since resided; after the death of his first wife he married Mrs. Eliza Buker, of Ellsworth; James, 3d, who lived on the land taken up by his grandfather; he resided for several years in the house now owned by Napoleon B. Trask, and later built the house he lived in at the time of his death; his wife was Harriet Gott; his death occurred in 1898, at the age of seventy years; Henry D., who built his house on the lot formerly owned by Mark Staples; he is a ship carpenter, and occupies the yard formerly used by Moses Staples, sr.; his wife was Louisa Staples; Oliver L., who had a part of his father's lot of land and who built his house nearly opposite his father's; his wife was Amanda, daughter of Augustus R. Staples; Levi B., who occupies the homestead lot; his wife was Matilda Staples. These five brothers lived in the same school district in which they were born, over half a century. In the year 1896 three of the family died. Asa died in Ellsworth, where he moved the year before, aged seventy-four years. Oliver L. died, aged sixty-two years, and Mrs. Mary Babbidge died in Rockland, aged seventy-eight years. There was one other son, Wellington, who died when a child.

William Joyce was born in 1802; he was the second son of James Joyce, sr. He lived on his father's place till after the latter's death. In 1848 he went back to Deer Isle, where he died. His farm became the property of James Joyce, 3d. He was the father of ten children, as follows: John B., born in 1821; died in 1840; Seth, born in 1823; lived at Deer Isle; William A., born in 1826; settled at North Haven; Elizabeth, wife of William Wood, born in 1831; Moses S., born in 1834; now resides at Deer Isle; Hannah, wife of William Hatch, of Oceanville, born in 1837; John, a second child by that name, born in 1840; Mary E., born in 1844; Justin A., born in 1846. Most of this family died at Deer Isle.

Ebenezer Joyce, another son of James Joyce, sr., built a house near where Charles H. Joyce's house now stands. He afterwards bought the lot taken up by Rev. Bryant Lennan, for which he paid $300; transfer was made May 24, 1826. This property is now occupied in part by Reuben Joyce. His wife was Catherine Stinson, a sister of his brother James's wife, also a sister of the wife of Alexander Staples. They were the three daughters of John Stinson, of Deer Isle. Mr. Joyce represented this town in the State legislature in 1859; he died in 1875, at the age of seventy-seven years. His wife died in 1886, aged eighty-three years. They were the parents of eleven children — six sons and five daughters. The daughters were: Sophrona, widow of Simeon Staples; resides in Rockland; Lucy, wife of Seth Staples; Rosalinda, wife of Capt. Stephen Babbidge, of Rockland; she is now dead; Augusta, wife of Elias Harrington, of Rockland; Melita, wife of Cyrus Gahan, of Rockland.

The sons were: Isaiah B., who married Olive Torrey; his place is now owned by David H. Sprague; he died in 1882, aged sixty-one years; Mrs. Joyce died in 1861, aged thirty-nine years; Roderick M., who married Catherine Stinson in 1847; he bought the house and lot of land of Asa Staples on Middle Head; he was extensively engaged in the fishing business at one time; he moved to Castine in 1864; his place is now owned by Michael Stinson; Eben S., who built the house where William S. Joyce now lives; his wife was Sarah Y. Stinson, whom he married in 1854; He died in 1894: John, who died in 1893 at Bluehill; Reuben, who occupies the homestead lot; his wife was Mary A. Lunt, of Long Island; after her death he married Mrs. Abbie Young, of Bluehill; William S., who resides on the place bought by his brother Eben; his wife was Deborah Bridges.

The last two brothers are the only ones of this family who now reside in this town.

Levi Torrey.

Levi Torrey took up a lot of one hundred acres adjoining the Joyce lot on the south. He came here from Deer Isle (where he was born in 1789) about 1814. He built a house on his lot which was situated to the south of where Winslow D. Stanley now lives. Mr. Torrey's father, Jonathan Torrey, came to Deer Isle in 1763 from Falmouth, Maine, and took up a tract of land of two hundred acres, near the north part of Deer Isle. He married, in 1767, a daughter of William Eaton, and after her death he married a Mrs. Robinson, who was a sister of Moses Staples, sr. He lost his life by the capsizing of a boat near Cape Rosier, while returning from Castine. His oldest son, David, was in the boat, and being more vigorous, was able to keep himself upon the boat's bottom, and for a while kept his father upon it with him; but as the water was cold he soon became chilled, fell off and was drowned. David was rescued. It has been stated that a certain man belonging to that town passed them when they were both upon the boat, but made no effort to save them. This man afterwards admitted that he saw them.

By his first wife Jonathan Torrey had five sons— David, born in 1768; William, whose widow married Amos Gordon; he was the father of Hezekiah Torrey, who represented the town of Deer Isle in the State legislature in 1822; William, who died on a passage from California around Cape Horn, and a daughter, who was the first wife of John P. Johnson. Another son was Capt.

Jonathan Torrey, born in 1774, who died of smallpox in 1847; the widow of his son David died in 1879, at the advanced age of ninety-seven years. There were also Francis H. and John, who lived and died at Newbury Neck, Surry.

By his second wife Jonathan Torrey had four sons—James, Levi, the subject of this sketch, Deacon Asa, who died in Ellsworth, and Capt. Ebenezer. Mr. Torrey also had three daughters by his first marriage, who were the wives of Nathan Haskell, Jonathan Eaton and Nathaniel Webster, who lived at Cape Elizabeth. The real estate of Mr. Torrey at Deer Isle is still owned by his descendants; the larger part of it was owned by the late Capt. Daniel S. Torrey, and is still occupied by his widow.

After coming to Swan's Island, Levi Torrey married Olive, daughter of James Joyce, sr. They were the parents of eleven children, six sons and five daughters. Mr. Torrey died in 1863, aged seventy-four years; his wife died in 1883, at the advanced age of ninety-two years.

Their daughters were: Louisa, wife of John Perkins, of Bluehill; Olive, wife of Isaiah B. Joyce, who died in 1861; Emily died when a child; Martha, wife of Freeman Torrey, of Tremont; after his death she became the third wife of Seth Stockbridge, of Rowley, Mass., and Miranda, wife of George Colter, who resided in Ellsworth.

The sons were: Joseph R., who bought a part of the Babbidge lot, and built the house now owned by Stephen Dunham, jr.; his wife was Roxalana Richardson, whom he married in 1839; they were the parents of two daughters — Louise, wife of Hardy Lane, of Sedgwick, and Emily, wife of Allen Reed, of Saccarappa; Mr. Torrey died in 1880, aged sixty-five years; his wife died in 1893, aged seventy-eight years; Capt. Levi, jr., who bought a part of the Mark Staples lot, and built a house where his son, Jefferson Torrey, now lives; in 1840 he married Joanna Staples; she died in 1887, aged sixty-six years; Mr. Torrey died in 1857, aged forty-one years. They were the parents of Andrew J., who died in 1888, at the age of forty-six years, Jefferson, Samuel and George; Lucretia, Clarinda and Olive; Charles, who married Ann Baker, and lived in Rockland; Ezra, who was drowned from a boat near his home in the year 1865; his wife was Susan Reed, who still occupies his property; Albert, who married Mary E. Dolliver, and resides at Tremont; Amaziah, who married Mary A. Nealey in 1857, and lives near Irish point.

Courtney Babbidge.

Courtney Babbidge came here from Deer Isle some time prior to the war of 1812, and took up the lot of land lying south of Mr. Torrey's. His wife was Mercy Joyce, a daughter of James Joyce, sr. Mr. Babbidge had lived here but a short time when he removed to Harrington, and later to West Trenton. He died in 1856, aged seventy-five years. Mrs. Babbidge died in 1865, aged eighty years. When Mr. Babbidge moved from this island he divided his property between his two sons, Joseph and Alfred; the latter sold his property to Joseph Torrey, who built the house now owned by Stephen Dunham, jr. Mr. and Mrs. Babbidge were the parents of eleven children— six sons and five daughters.

The daughters were: Ruth, who was born at Deer Isle, wife of Eben Jordan, of Harrington, and settled there; Abbie, who was born at Swan's Island; she became the wife of John Smith, and settled first at Deer Isle; later they moved to West Trenton; Mercy, wife of Levi B. Crockett, of Deer Isle; Sarah, wife of Thomas Haynes, settled at West Trenton; Mary, born at Harrington, was the wife of Nathan McRay, of Orange, N. J., where they settled.

The sons were: Alfred, born at Deer Isle; he married Hannah Hamblen and settled at Swan's Island: he lived for some time in a house over an old cellar still seen near the road south of David H. Sprague's, and after his father's removal from this place, Alfred occupied a part of his property. Their children were Alfred, Stephen, Martha, Augustus and Melinda. Mr. Babbidge afterwards moved to Rockland. While sailing from this port he died at sea. After the death of his wife he married Susan Perry.

Joseph S., born at Deer Isle in 1806; he married Mary C. Hamblen, and settled on the lot now owned by Augustus W. Staples; he died in 1883, aged seventy-six years; Mrs. Babbidge died in 1881, aged seventy-one years. Their children were Daniel H., who was lost in the schooner "Constitution" off Nausett light, Cape Cod, in 1860, at the age of twenty-eight years; his widow,

Emily (Reed), afterward became the wife of Capt. Winthrop Lane; she was drowned by the foundering of the vessel "S. J. Collins" on their way home from Boston, together with all on board, among whom were Mrs. Lane, two children, Lillian Babbidge, aged eight years, and Grace Lane, one year; Joseph, who married Isabella Murphy; he died of smallpox at Mount Desert; Martin V., who has often served on the school board in this town; he represented this district in the legislature in 1876; Hannah A., wife of Capt. Benjamin J. Staples.

The other sons of Courtney Babbidge who did not reside here were John, who married Isabella Strout, and settled at Harrington; Courtney, jr., who was born at Swan's Island, married Lucy Leighton, and settled at Harrington, afterwards moving to Boston; William, who married Susan York, of Ellsworth, where he settled; he afterwards moved to Dakota; Samuel, who married Sarah ———, and settled in Norwich, Conn.

The grandfather of Courtney Babbidge, also Courtney, came to Deer Isle in 1773 from Windham, Maine. He was three times married; his last wife was a Miss Staples, who after her husband's death, became the wife James Joyce, sr. Mr. Babbidge's sons were Stephen, Courtney, James and William; his daughters were the two wives of Oliver Lane, and of Capt. Hezekiah Colby.

Of the sons, James removed to Vinalhaven, where he lived and died; William settled at Windham; Courtney was a Revolutionary soldier, and is said to have been present at the surrender of Cornwallis; he sold his farm at Deer Isle and removed to a small island at the entrance to Fox Island thoroughfare, still known as Babbidge's island; he died there in 1834.

The other son of Mr. Babbidge, sr., was Stephen, the father of the subject of this sketch. Stephen's wife was Hannah Staples, a sister of Moses Staples, sr. His children were: Courtney, who, as we have noticed, settled on Swan's Island; Stephen; Levi, a master mariner; John, who died suddenly in 1826; Aaron; William; James, who, in 1833, was drowned with his wife and child in passing through the flood gates into the mill pond at Southeast Harbor, Deer Isle. The daughters were the wives of William Barter, of Isle au Haut, and Nathaniel Robbins. Mr. Robbins is still living (1898) in his ninety-eighth year.

Stephen Babbidge, sr., died in 1841, aged eighty-two years. He was for many years an invalid; he was much respected, and in his day had considerable influence at Deer Isle, and acquired much property. After the death of his wife he married her sister, Mrs. Saunders, and afterwards, in 1835, married the widow of Stephen Dow.

John Cook.

John Cook came here near the year 1799. He was a Welshman and together with one of his countrymen, Charles Chatto, and two Irishmen, Michael Ready and John Finney, were in the military service of Great Britain from which they deserted and came to Deer Isle. They were stationed near the St. Croix river, and either by swimming, or in a boat, they came alongside of a vessel belonging to Deer Isle, the master of which was Capt. Ephraim Marshall, who, on hearing of the hardships they were forced to endure, kindly consented to let them remain aboard and brought them to Deer Isle. Mr. Chatto, who married a Miss Staples, and Mr. Ready, who married Lydia Pressey, remained at Deer Isle until their death. Mr. Cook and Mr. Finney, whom we shall notice later, settled on this island.

Mr. Cook married, at Deer Isle, Zeruah, widow of Joshua Staples, and a daughter of John Raynes, sr., who came to Deer Isle in 1772, from York, Maine. By her first marriage she had one daughter, Jane, who became the wife of Elias Morey, jr. They subsequently came here to live. Mr. Cook took up a tract of land lying to the west of the Joyce and Torrey lots. It contained eighty-seven acres. He built a log house which he occupied until 1835. Mrs. Cook had no children by her second marriage. In his later years, being able no longer to perform manual labor, he had Elias Morey, jr., whose wife was Mrs. Cook's daughter by her first marriage, come and live with them. Mr. Cook died in 1846. His wife died a few years before; both attained a great age.

Elias Morey, Jr.

Elias Morey, jr., came here from Deer Isle in 1832, and moved upon the lot with Mr. Cook, which place he afterwards came into possession of. Mr. Morey's wife, as has been stated, was Jane Staples. Before coming here

Morey lived on what is known as the Ring farm at Mountainville, Deer Isle; the farm then, in 1822, belonged to Spofford and Towne. Morey's grandfather, Ezekiel Morey, came to Deer Isle from Meadow's river, near Brunswick, in 1787, and built the first frame house on Deer Isle. He was twice married and was the father of thirteen children. The sons who survived him were Elias, Ezekiel, Isaac, Joseph and James. The first-named son was the father of the subject of this sketch.

When Mr. Morey came here the lands he occupied were covered with a heavy timber growth, which he cut off and sold for kiln-wood. Mrs. Morey died in 1854, at the age of sixty-three years. After her death Mr. Morey married Sarah L. Friend, of Sedgwick, an estimable lady, who died in 1889, in her ninety-first year. His death occurred in 1867, aged seventy-six years. By his first marriage Mr. Morey had five children — three daughters and two sons.

The daughters were: Martha, wife of Asa C. Staples; she died in 1866, aged fifty years; Jane, wife of Calvin P. Abbott; they lived in Hancock; Mr. Abbott went on foreign voyages, and died while at the West Indies, where he was buried: after this Mrs. Abbott came here and lived with her father until her death, which occurred in 1851, at the age of thirty-three years; Lois, wife of James Sprague; she died in 1885, aged sixty-four years.

The sons were: Otis, who resided at Mt. Desert; his wife was Elizabeth Reed; after her death he married

Matilda Closson; he died in 1886; Hezekiah, who in 1867 came into possession of his father's property; he built a house to the west of his father's; his wife was Nancy A. Conary, daughter of Israel Conary, whom he married in 1845.

Mr. Morey, by great industry and economy, acquired considerable property. He died in 1885, at the age of sixty-one years. His real estate is owned by John Stanley. Mrs. Morey moved to Winterport in 1897.

Rev. Bryant Lennan.

Rev. Bryant Lennan, a minister of the Baptist denomination, came in 1814 from Hampden, and took up the lot south of the Morey lot, which extended to the shore on the northwest; it is the Stockbridge lot, and included the land now owned by Reuben Joyce and David H. Sprague. He built a house on what is now known as Stockbridge hill, and later built one near where Reuben Joyce now lives. He was the first settled minister on this island. He organized the Baptist society here. According to the record of Eastern Maine Baptist association holden in Sedgwick, October 11, 1820. the Swan's Island Baptist church was taken into the association at that time with a membership of twenty-three. Among the representatives from this place, as delegates at this and subsequent meetings, as appears in those old records, were the names of Joshua Staples, Courtney Babbidge, Deacon James Joyce and Ebenezer Joyce. The first two years Mr. Lennan preached here he was only a licensed preacher, but on

October 2, 1822 he was ordained. He was married when he came here, and had a family but none of them settled in this town.

Mr. Lennan was a well-educated man, very earnest and faithful in the performance of his ministerial duties, and was much respected by the people. He remained here several years. He then went back to Hampden, and his land was purchased by Ebenezer Joyce and John Stockbridge. Some fifteen years after leaving here, after the death of his wife, he came back and preached several years, after which time we have no further record of him.

John Stockbridge.

John Stockbridge came here from Deer Isle in 1816. He lived for several years on a place formerly owned by Alfred Babbidge, south of where David H. Sprague now lives. When Elder Lennan moved away he bought the eastern half of his land, and lived many years in a log house that Mr. Lennan built. He afterward built a frame house on this lot where he lived the remainder of his life.

Mr. Stockbridge's father, Capt. Benjamin Stockbridge, came to Deer Isle from Gloucester, Mass. He was a shipmaster in good circumstances. It is said he was in the ship that first carried the American flag up the Dardanelles; it was in the year 1800 that the frigate "George Washington" displayed the star-spangled banner before the crescent beneath the walls of Constantinople. It was the occasion of the bearing of tribute from the Dey of Algiers to the Sultan. When the stars and stripes appeared at the Bosphorus, the people did not know what the flag represented, or, in fact, anything about it, and in order to pass the forts and castles the captain resorted to an admirable stratagem. When the "George Washington" neared the forts her commander shortened sail, and made ready to anchor; as he did so he ordered a salute fired, which was quickly responded to by the batteries of the fort. The scene was soon shrouded in dense smoke, and when it cleared away the astonished Turks saw that the frigate had taken advantage of the smoky veil to glide through the narrow strait, and was already far on her way to Constantinople.

After coming to Deer Isle he continued to follow the sea. He was a member of the Baptist church there, and it is said that when some difficulty occurred between him and some of his neighbors — members of the same church — an examination was made before the church. Capt. Stockbridge read to them the thirtieth chapter of Job, beginning: "But now they that are younger than I have me in derision, whose father I would have disdained to have set with the dogs of my flock."

Mr. Stockbridge when young was a man of energy and capacity, but in his latter years became somewhat reduced in circumstances. He had a family of eight children, six of whom were daughters. One was the wife of James Duncan; another the wife of John Greenlaw, who died in 1870, at the age of eighty-seven years, having lived in wedlock sixty-six years; the other daughters were the wives of Benjamin Lane, James Greenlaw, Capt. William Grover, of Isle au Haut, who later moved to Islesboro, and the wife of George Grover. There were two sons — Benjamin, who was lost at sea when a young man, and John, the subject of this sketch. He came here when a young man, and married Ruth, daughter of James Joyce, sr. Mr. Stockbridge was an intelligent man, and much respected. Most of the early records of the plantation were made by him, he having been chosen the first clerk in 1834; he held the office for many years. He died in 1859, aged sixty-three years. Ruth, his wife, died the year before, at the age of sixty-nine years. They were the parents of nine children — two daughters, Sarah, wife of Albert Smith, of Ellsworth, and Mercy, wife of Gilman Staples, and seven sons, as follows:

Benjamin, born in 1817. He built the house where Benjamin, jr., now lives. He married, in 1842, Sarah Norwood, by whom he had four children — Isaiah, Mary E., wife of Charles H. Joyce, James E. and Benjamin W., all of whom reside here. Mr. Stockbridge is dead; his widow still resides here.

John married Hannah M. Murphy, and after her death, which occurred in 1864, at the age of thirty-six years, he married Susan Morey, of Deer Isle. Mr. Stockbridge represented this town in the State legislature in 1867. He died in 1881, aged sixty-two years. Mrs. Stockbridge afterwards became the wife of Thomas Pinkham, of Boothbay.

James, born in 1818. He was taken ill while aboard

a ship, and was taken to New York, where he died in Bellevue hospital in 1843, at the age of twenty-five years. He was unmarried.

Samuel W. married, in 1852, Martha Finney, and they were the parents of six children. He died in 1883, aged sixty-two years.

Deacon Seth W. went to Gloucester when a young man, and for a time went in fishing vessels from that port. He was next promoted to captain of a freighting schooner employed in carrying fresh halibut from Gloucester to Boston. Later he engaged in buying and shipping fresh halibut, in company with William T. Smith and William Rackcliffe, at what is now Walen's wharf, and on the decease of his partners admitted David L. Robinson into the firm. On the formation of the Atlantic Halibut Co. he was an original stockholder. While here engaged he did a large business, and owned extensively in shipping. After having been engaged in active business for nearly half a century, he bought a fine farm in Rowley, Mass., where he spent the greater part of the later years of his life. He was three times married; his first wife was Eliza I. Kiff, of East Gloucester, to whom he was married in 1851. After her death he married, in 1865, his first wife's sister, Mrs. Nancy Elwell. She died in 1884 at Rowley, after which he married Mrs. Martha Torrey, who survives him. He owned a cottage at Swan's Island, where he usually spent a part of the year. He died in 1896 at Rowley, at the age of seventy years.

Eben lives in Gloucester. His wife was Clarissa Kiff, a sister of the two first wives of his brother Seth W.

William was the youngest son. He married Fannie Thurston, of Tremont. He was an architect, and worked at his trade in Boston and Beverly; at the latter place he died.

John Finney.

John Finney bought the lot adjoining Moses Staples, sr., on the south, being the land just vacated by William Davis. He was a native of Ireland, and was in the military service of Great Britain. While stationed near the St. Croix river he deserted and came aboard of a vessel belonging to Deer Isle. This vessel was commanded by Capt. Ephraim Marshall, who, together with John Cook and others of the same company, came to Deer Isle in 1799. There he married the eldest daughter of Moses Staples, sr. He came to Swan's Island in 1803, and bought the tract of land already described. He built three houses in different locations. The first house stood near the shore, where Jefferson Torrey now resides; the second was near the back shore, and the third to the south of Moses Staples. Mr. Finney was small of stature and of a rather excitable disposition, but he was ever ready to defend a cause he considered just. After the death of his wife Mr. Finney lived with his son until the death of the latter's wife, when he moved to Somesville, where he died in 1844. When Mr. Finney left he sold his property here to Moses Staples, 3d, and it is now owned by Gilman

Staples. Mr. and Mrs. Finney were the parents of nine children.

The daughters were: Nancy, wife of Choate Barton; Mary A., wife of Reuben Remick, of Ellsworth; Sally, wife of Edward Courts, of Boston; Eliza died unmarried; Dorcas, wife of Oliver Eaton, of Sedgwick.

The sons were: Moses S., who married Eliza Stinson; he lived here with his father for several years; after the death of his wife, in 1838, he went to Deer Isle and married Margaret, widow of John Buckminster; he died Dec. 11, 1860, aged fifty-eight years; he was the first person buried in the cemetery at Oceanville: Thomas, who married Lydia Gott, of Mount Desert, where he resided: John, who married in Boston.

Peter Gott.

Peter Gott, one of the most interesting characters of eastern Maine, took up the tract south of Moses Staples, or the point of land to Hocomock Head. This is now owned and occupied by the descendants of Isaiah L. Stanley and others. Peter is said to have been a cousin of Daniel Gott, who owned Gott's Island, and after whom it was named. This Gott family came from Cape Ann, at which place there are still many of that name.

Peter came to this State previous to the Revolutionary war, and settled at Ship Harbor, a small inlet east of Bass Harbor, and later moved to Swan's Island, where he reared his family. He married, near the year 1776, Charity Kain, by whom he had eleven children, born between the years 1777 and 1799: I have been able to trace only nine; the other two presumably died young. After coming here he built a house near where the widow of Isaiah L. Stanley now lives.

After the death of his wife Charity, and the accidental drowning of Daniel Gott, of Gott's Island, with two sons, David and Charles, Peter married, in 1824, the widow. He then sold his place here to his son-in-law, William Stanley, and moved to Gott's Island, where he lived many years until after the death of his second wife, when he came back to Swan's Island, where he remained until his death, which occurred in 1839. He was over eighty years of age. He was buried in the little cemetery near Hocomock Head.

The Gott family spread far and wide among the early settlers, and has left its particular and distinctive features on the people of these islands down to the present time. A rough and hardy people, vigorous and tough; they have continually intermarried, and the family to-day differs in many respects from its vigorous ancestors. The following nine children of Peter and Charity Gott reached adult age; there were seven daughters and two sons; the daughters were:

(1) Mary, wife of Thomas Trevitt; (2) Eunice, wife of Asa Conary, of Bluehill; her children were Alvin, Asa, Belinda and Augusta Conary: (3) Margaret, wife of Jonathan Rich, of Bass Harbor: Mr. Rich died in 1817, aged thirty-seven years; her children were John Rich, who married Rhoda Dodge and settled at Bass Har-

bor; Robert Rich married Ann Bushee; Samuel Rich married Clarissa Gally; Maurice Rich married Data Peters, of Bass Harbor; Zebadiah Rich married Eunice Robbins, of Tremont; Lydia Rich married John Smith and settled on Swan's Island; Amy Rich married William Nutter, whom we shall notice, and Lucy Rich married James Marsh; (4) Ruth Gott married William Stanley; (5) Lydia Gott married Mark Staples; these last two married and settled on this island, and their families have been considered elsewhere; (6) Patience Gott married [1] Morris Peters, [2] James Camel, [3] James York; by her first husband her children were Data, Betsy, Mary, Calvert and James Peters; (7) Charity Gott married William Rich and settled on Outer Long Island, where they have many descendants.

Capt. John Gott, the oldest son of Peter and Charity Gott, married, in 1798, Ruth Barton, of Castine. They lived at Ship Harbor for several years, where some of their children were born. He was for many years a master mariner. He came here and took up the tract of land adjoining Joshua Grindle on the northeast; it includes the whole lot from where Horace E. Stanley now lives to David H. Sprague's land, and went to the brook north of Ambrose Gott's. He built a house where Albion Smith's barn now stands. When quite an old man he abandoned the sea, and began to cultivate his farm. But he was induced to make one more voyage which proved to be his last. A party of nine young men from Sedgwick or near there, secured a vessel commanded by Capt. John Gordon to go on a fishing trip. The captain, being young and inexperienced, came to this island for a pilot to accompany them on this voyage. After much urging Capt. Gott consented to accompany them. They left for Green Bank. When a few days out a terrible storm came up, and it is supposed they foundered at sea, as they were never heard from. This was near the year 1840. Capt. Gott's age was about seventy years. After his death his widow married Abraham Kingsland, of Kingsland Landing, New York city. It is said he was heir to a valuable tract of land in that city, and had affidavits to prove his claim, but while intoxicated these were gotten from him. Repeated efforts were made to recover these papers, but without avail. In after years he left here to go to New York, where he was to live with his children by a former marriage, but he never arrived there. A man answering his description was found dead in Portland, and it was thought he met his death while under the influence of liquor, to which he was addicted. His death occurred about the year 1859. Mr. Gott's property went to his son Joseph, except what was known as the Babbidge lot, which was owned by Edward Gott. Mrs. Kingsland died in Rockland in 1865, aged eighty-four years.

The children of Mr. and Mrs. Gott were: Martha, wife of Israel Conary; Prudence, wife of John Foster; after his death she became the wife of Samuel Irving, an Englishman; both her husbands belonged in Boston; after she became a widow the second time, she moved to Palermo, where she died; Ruth, wife of William Fife;

she died in 1844, aged twenty-eight years. The sons were John, David, Samuel, Joseph, Edward and Ambrose; three other children, Samuel, Hiram and Sally, died young. These children, most of whom settled here, will be further considered.

Martha Gott married Israel Conary, and settled on the lot known as City point; he afterwards moved to Black Island, where he lived several years; he finally came back here, and bought a part of the Gott lot, then owned by Joseph Gott, and built the house where David Stanley now lives. This family is noticed in another place.

John Gott married Abigail Merchant and settled where the widow of Daniel Bridges now lives, and to whom Mr. Gott sold his place when the latter went to Rockland. Mr. Gott died in 1875, aged seventy-nine years. His wife died in 1874, aged eighty-two years. Their children were: Harriet, wife of James Joyce, 3d; Prudence, wife of William Smith; Mary, wife of Wilbert Boynton; David, who married Jane Ingraham: Caroline, wife of John Ham. The last three settled in Rockland.

David Gott married Clara Winthrop, of Palermo. They were the parents of three children. He died in 1877.

Samuel Gott married Mary Merchant. His children were Mary, Lydia, Samuel, William, Roxana and Eudora, all of whom are dead except Lydia. After the death of his wife, Mr. Gott, in 1852, married Barbara M. Carter, of Brooklin. By this wife he had several children, of whom Augusta and Fred live here. His second wife died in 1895, aged sixty-two years.

Joseph Gott bought the lot at City point of Israel Conary. He built a house on the east side of the road nearly opposite where Verenus Reed now lives. His wife was Eunice Sprague, by whom he had the following children: Manley and Susan, who died young; Rodney, who married Nancy Joyce, and now resides in Somerville, Mass.; Freeman, who married Mary Stinson; Augusta, wife of Capt. William P. Herrick; Leroy, who died in the civil war; Fred, who married Hannah Gott; Harris, who married Diantha Bridges; Myra, wife of Hardy Stinson.

Edward Gott settled on a part of the lot first taken up by Joshua Grindle, and which is now owned by Horace E. Stanley. His wife was Susan Staples, a daughter of Moses Staples, 2d; she died in 1895, aged seventy-seven. Mr. Gott's death occurred in 1885, at the age of seventy years. They were the parents of eleven children, as follows: Gilbert J., who married Mary Carter, of Sedgwick; he was lost at sea February 10, 1860, at the age of twenty-three years; Susan F., who is now a resident of Boston; Pathena J., wife of Hezekiah Holbrook; Martha, wife of Charles W. Kent; Edward Warren, drowned November 6, 1869, aged twenty-three; Lucy A. married John Beal, of Deer Isle, and now resides in Bucksport; Hattie A., wife of Horace E. Stanley; Emma R., wife of James E. Kent, of Addison; Delora A., wife of Leaman D. Bridges; she died February 17, 1882, aged twenty-seven; Mary E., wife of Thomas J. Stanley; Mina M., unmarried, is in the millinery business at Bath.

Ambrose Gott had his father's lot at City point. His wife was Sarah A. Herrick, with whom he lived in wedlock over half a century. He died in 1894, aged seventy years. His widow still occupies the place. Their children were Aurilla, Ellen, Alice, Hannah, Clara, Joseph, Alvarado, John and Emery.

Peter Gott, jr., the second and last son of Peter and Charity Gott, settled at Bass Harbor. His wife was Puah Richardson. Their children were Alpheus, who was drowned with his father in a great gale off Cape Ann; Benjamin; William; Martha, wife of Joseph Gott, settled at Goose Cove; Betsey, who married a Mr. Kent; Joanna, wife of William Tinker; Lydia M., wife of William Scott Richardson, of Bluehill.

Cushing Stewart.

Cushing Stewart came here from North Haven in 1822, and took up the lot south of Benjamin Smith. It is the land now owned by his son, George Stewart, and the Rowe estate. He built a house near Spirit cove. Mr. Stewart was born at Fox Island in 1797 and was of Scotch parentage. He served through the war of 1812. After coming home from the war, he married Ann Robinson, of Mount Desert, where he lived several years previous to coming here, and where his first two children were born. He died in 1838 at the age of forty-one years. His death occurred in Rockland while on board a vessel. After his death Mrs. Stewart became, in 1840, the wife of Abel Lane, who came here from Deer Isle. Mr. Lane lived here for some years, then moved to Brooklin, where he died about the year 1874. After his death Mrs. Lane returned to this town and lived with her daughter until Mrs. Lane's death. Mr. and Mrs. Stewart were the parents of five children.

The daughters were: Elvira, wife of Samuel Robinson, of Gouldsboro; Mary, wife of James Smith; Cordelia, widow of James Rowe; he came here from Baldwin, and settled on a part of the Stewart lot; Mr. Rowe died in 1891, aged sixty-nine years.

The sons were: Otis, who married Louisa Marshall, of Islesboro, and afterwards moved to Georgetown; George, who married Elizabeth Robinson; he now lives here on the homestead lot.

Benjamin Stinson.

Benjamin Stinson came to this place from Deer Isle near 1810. His grandfather, Thomas Stinson, was the first settler on that part of Deer Isle called Stinson's Neck and after whom that place was named. He came there from Woolwich in 1773. It is said that he held the first religious services ever held in Deer Isle; its occasion was the regret of his wife that they could not have the religious privileges that they enjoyed in Woolwich. So the next Sunday Mr. Stinson, accompanied by his family, went to the shade of a large tree that grew near his house, and performed the services usual on such occasions — reading a sermon. He was the first justice of the peace on Deer Isle, and was a man of integrity and had considerable influence. He had a large family, one of whom was William Stinson, the father of the subject of this sketch. Another son was Samuel Stinson, who was a Revolutionary soldier. William married Miss York, by whom he had his family; after her death he married Polly Calef, and after her death he married the widow of William Webb. William, as well as his father, was deacon of the Congregational church for many years.

Benjamin, the subject of this sketch, was born in 1778. He came here and took up a tract of two hundred and forty acres of land near Seal Cove. This property is now owned by Call and Dyer. Here he built a log house and later a frame house. In 1811 he married Sarah B. Smith, a daughter of David Smith, sr., whom we have noticed was born in 1792 on Harbor island, being the first white child born there. He afterwards bought the tract of land first taken up by Moses Staples, sr., which extended from William Stanley's to the Grindle lot. Previous to buying this last lot he had moved to Exeter, Maine, but he soon returned. Later he exchanged lots with his son John, and lived where Daniel McKay now resides. His farm at Seal Cove was divided between his two sons, John and David.

Mr. Stinson was one of the early justices of the peace here. He represented Swan's Island and Mount Desert in the State legislature in 1837. For several years he was a master mariner. Mr. Stinson was a well-informed man, very decided in his views, and fond of discussing any subject. When he came here there were no public schools, and no municipal organization. He was foremost in getting this island organized as a plantation, which was accomplished in 1834, and he was tireless in his efforts to establish public schools — a most worthy undertaking for which he should long be remembered. He also was the means of having a post-office established here, and he was appointed the first postmaster. Previous to this time there had been no regular mails or any place to receive them. Mails were sent and brought by any boat that chanced to go to the main land. He was in all a public-spirited man, and worked for the public benefit of his adopted town, an example which, if more generally practiced at the present time, would result in much benefit now as well as to future generations.

Mr. Stinson died in 1867, aged eighty-nine years. His wife died in 1856, aged sixty-four years. They were the parents of ten children — five sons and five daughters, all of whom lived to adult age. The sons were: Rev. Benjamin F., born in 1812; John, born in 1815; William, born in 1817; David, born in 1821; Capt. Michael, born in 1833. The daughters were: Livonia, born in 1819, was the wife of Hardy Lane; Keturah, born in 1823, was the wife of Oliver Lane; Catherine was born in 1825, and was the wife of Roderick Joyce; she died in 1893, aged sixty-eight years. Sarah, born in 1827, was the wife of Eben Joyce; she died in 1855, aged fifty-eight years; Mary, born in 1832, married George Hemmingway, of Chelsea. The sons will be further considered.

I. *Rev. Benjamin F. Stinson*, the oldest child of the family, was born in 1812. He attended the common school, and later the Maine Wesleyan seminary at Kent's Hill, where he prepared to enter the ministry in the service of the Methodist church. He married Hannah, daughter of Moses Staples, 2d. He occupied the place that his father had bought of Moses Staples, sr., and built a house where his brother, Capt. Michael Stinson, now lives. For several years he traded, doing a good business, and having an extensive trade. During the time he was trading there was no other store on the island. He also owned quite extensively in shipping. His store was located on the site now owned by S. Morse.

His methods of doing business were rather slack for his own benefit, and he soon went out of business. He then devoted his whole time in the service of the church, and was ordained about the year 1862. While belonging to the conference he preached at Deer Isle, Tremont, Addison, Hancock and other places. During the declining years of his life he settled down at Tremont, where he bought a farm belonging to Rev. Charles Brown. He preached at Tremont and Swan's Island alternate Sundays, often coming here in an open boat; he would subject himself to any exposure or inconvenience to meet an appointment. He was an earnest, faithful worker, and for his time was considered a good preacher, much beloved by those with whom he labored. A Methodist church recently erected at Gott's Island has been dedicated to his memory for the faithful services rendered it. While here he was often honored by offices of trust in the town affairs. He represented this town in the State legislature in 1855. His death occurred in 1887, at the age of seventy-five years. His wife died at Swan's Island in 1895, at the age of eighty-five years. She was the last survivor of a large family.

II. *John Stinson* settled on that part of the Grindle lot now owned by Daniel McKay, and he built the house now standing there. His wife was Lucy Smith, by whom he had the following children: Nelson, who married Mary Reed, and who now resides in Harpswell; Meletiah J., who married Viola Rowe; after his death she became the wife of Byron Morse, who died in 1897; Deborah, wife of Leroy Smith; she died in Belfast in 1896; Charlotte, wife of Frank Gott. Several other children died young. As already stated, John exchanged places with his father, and, together with his brother David, went to Seal Cove. They both lived in their father's house there for some years. Later they divided the lot of land, John building the house now owned by Henry B. Call, and David built the house now owned by Mr. Dyer. Mr. Stinson died in 1852, aged thirty-seven years.

III. *William Stinson* bought a part of Harbor island, and built the house that now stands there. This island is still owned by his heirs and by Capt. Michael Stinson. He married Elizabeth Lane, of Deer Isle. After her death he married Lizzie, daughter of Billings

Hardy, of Freeze's island. He died in 1890, aged seventy-three years. His children were: Sarah, wife of John Hardy, of Frankfort; Hardy and Oliver, who now reside in Boston.

IV. *Capt. Michael Stinson* is the only one of this family who resides in this town. In 1859 he married Naomi G. Whitney, of Shelburne, Nova Scotia. He was for many years a successful master mariner. He also did considerable business in trade.

Enoch Billings.

Enoch Billings came here from Sedgwick in 1826, and took up the tract of land north of David Smith. It contained one hundred and seventy-five acres, and is known as the "Narrows lot". This place was afterwards bought by James Smith, and at present is owned by J. T. Crippen, of Ellsworth. On it are located some valuable stone quarries. Mr. Billings' wife was Sarah Carter, whom he married in Sedgwick previous to his coming here. She was a large, powerful woman, often performing feats of strength that would have done credit to a man.

Most of their children were born in Sedgwick; they were Enoch, who was afflicted with epileptic fits: one day while fishing in a boat, he had an epileptic seizure, fell from the boat, and was drowned; his boat was found anchored; John, another son, lived here for some years, and afterwards moved to Brewer, where he bought a large farm, and there he died; his wife was Harriet Billings; Johnson, another son, was born in Sedgwick in 1810, and came here with his father; he married Eliza Smith, a daughter of David Smith, sr.; he built a house over a cellar north of where Capt. John C. Kent now lives; this place he sold to Asa Smith when he moved to Stinson's Neck, Deer Isle, where he bought the farm near the school-house. Mr. Billings was an industrious man, and lived in easy circumstances; he is now living, in his ninety-first year, hale and vigorous; his wife died in 1891, aged seventy-seven years.

The daughters of Enoch Billings were Edna, wife of Thomas Conary, of Surry, and Sarah, wife of Lovan Conary, of Surry. William and David Carter, brothers of Mrs. Enoch Billings, lived for some time here. William was drowned from a boat while coming from Deer Isle. David in after years moved away. They were both unmarried.

John Valentine.

John Valentine came here from East Haddam, Conn., in 1852, and married the widow of John Stinson, on whose place he lived while here. They afterwards moved to Rockland, where Mrs. Valentine died. Their children were Ann, who married a Mr. Manson in Massachusetts; Betsey and John, jr., also married in that state; the latter afterwards moved to Pennsylvania, and with him his father now resides.

Thomas Colomy.

Thomas Colomy came here from Damariscotta in 1823, he being then only eighteen years of age. He made his first visit to the island while in a fishing vessel. Afterwards he came and lived for several years with the family of Samuel Kent. His wife was Mercy Kent, whom he married soon after coming here. He bought the land and built a house near where David Smith now lives. This place he sold at the solicitation of a friend and bought Conary's island near Deer Isle, but in this purchase he was greatly deceived; the condition of this place was so much different from what he had been led to expect that he soon came back here and bought the place of William Annis, where Hezekiah Holbrook now lives. Previous to going to Conary's island he sold his farm here to David Smith, 3d, who still occupies it. After living on the Annis place some years, he moved to Irish point and bought the place then owned by David Stinson, next adjoining the Smith lot, where he spent the remainder of his years. He died in 1884, at the age of seventy-nine years. Mrs. Colomy died in 1879, aged fifty-nine years. They were the parents of ten children, most of whom have moved from this town.

The daughters were: Roxana, wife of Joseph Whitmore; Caroline, wife of Joel Whitmore, both of Deer Isle; these two daughters now reside in California; Lizzie, wife of Capt. Courtney Crockett, of Deer Isle; he was lost at sea in 1883 in the schooner "J. H. Miller", while he was on a voyage to Boston where he was to sell his vessel; this was to be his last trip to sea; his widow still resides at Oceanville; Lorenia, wife of William Sullivan, of Nova Scotia; they reside at Deer Isle; Margaret, Marietta and an infant died young.

The sons were: Franklin, who married Mary Whitmore; Edwin, who married Carrie Whitmore, both of Deer Isle, where they now reside; Hiram J., who was the only one of the family who settled here; he owned the place formerly occupied by his father at Irish point; his wife was Eva Smith; Mr. Colomy was drowned from an open boat Oct. 10, 1894; he started to row out from Seal Cove around Irish point in the face of a furious gale. It was raining very hard, rendering his frail boat very slippery, and it is supposed that in trying to change his position in the boat he slipped and fell into the water; his brother coming from Deer Isle in a boat picked up his empty boat and towed it into Old Harbor; he was forty-nine years of age.

Kimball Herrick.

Kimball Herrick came to this island and bought the John Smith place at Irish point, in 1839. His father was Eben Herrick, of Brooklin, one of the pioneer settlers there. His mother's maiden name was Priscilla Bridges. He had eight children. The daughters were: Allie, Emmeline, Hannah and Matilda; the sons were: Walter, Shadrich, Elijah, and Kimball, the subject of our sketch; they are now all dead.

Kimball was born in Brooklin in 1803, where he lived until after his marriage. His wife was Abigail M. Babson. Previous to his coming here he lived three years on Marshall's island, but he never owned any property there. Mr. Herrick died in 1887, aged eighty-four years. His wife died in 1884, aged eighty years. They were the parents of three daughters, all of whom are living here. They are Sarah A., widow of Ambrose Gott; Sapphira, widow of Isaiah L. Stanley; Abbie, wife of Abram Holbrook.

Samuel Kent.

Samuel Kent came here in 1805 from Annisquam, Mass., and for a number of years lived with his brother-in-law, Alexander Nutter, whose place he had when Mr. Nutter moved away. His place is what is now known as the Irish point farm.

The Kents are a very old family in this country. Three brothers came here from England in 1630, and landed in Portsmouth, N. H. Tradition says that in England they were in hiding five years to escape being beheaded during the reign of Charles I. They finally escaped and came to this country. Three brothers, Charles, Martin and Daniel, descendants of these Kents, came to this State from Marshfield, Mass., in 1793, and settled what has since been known as Kent's Hill, the location of the Maine Wesleyan seminary and female college. The Marshfield records also give the name of Samuel Kent, who married in 1728, Desire Baker, and in 1731 they had a son, also Samuel. Another of this family, Thomas Kent, settled near Gloucester in 1649. He had two sons, John and Samuel; the latter was married in 1654. He also had a son Samuel, born in 1661. This family being the only Kent family recorded as ever settling on Cape Ann, was undoubtedly the ancestor of the Mr. Kent who came to this town. The names given to his children here are but a repetition of the names of the Kent family on Cape Ann. This custom of naming children for family relatives was then almost universal. There are many Kents now living in or near Gloucester, and many of their descendants are scattered through Maine.

Mr. Kent married before coming here Katie Woolens, of Gloucester. They were the parents of nine children. Mr. Kent was drowned about the year 1831, while coming from Deer Isle in an open boat, where he had been to get Richard Warren to perform the marriage ceremony for his son Samuel. He accidentally fell overboard; a strong breeze was blowing, and before assistance could be rendered he had become exhausted and was drowned. His wife died in 1838. His property afterwards fell into the hands of ex-Governor Edward Kent, of Bangor, and was afterwards sold to John Smith and Kimball Herrick. Their daughters were: Abigail, wife of Asa Smith; Asenath, wife of a Mr. Smith, of Boston, where they reside; Mercy, wife of Thomas Colomy, who died in 1875, aged fifty-nine years; Catherine, who married in New York city. The sons were:

I. *Benjamin*, who was born in 1801, in Annisquam. His wife was Ann Smith, by whom he had five children. The daughters were: Sabrina, wife of John Wallace, of Jonesport; Sarah, wife of John Dobbin; Mercy, wife of Levi Alley. The sons were: David, who married

Elvira Wallace; John, who married a Mrs. Alley. The whole family settled at Jonesport.

II. *Samuel* was the second son. He was born in Annisquam in 1803; his wife was Mary, daughter of David Smith, sr. Mr. Kent, with George Smith, bought the Billings lot and built the house where Charles W. Kent now lives. They were the parents of six children— Eliza, Henrietta, Charles W., John Calvin, James E. and Hosea M. Mr. Kent died in 1877, aged seventy-four years. Mrs. Kent died in 1897, at the age of eighty-five years. The only survivor of the family of David Smith, sr., is Mrs. Kent's sister, Dorothy, wife of Benjamin Smith, 2d.

III. *James*, another son, married Rebecca Stower, of Gouldsboro. They settled in Brooklin where they died.

IV. *Martin*, in 1844, married Lois Billings. They resided in Sedgwick. He was a master mariner.

V. *Hiram* married, in 1848, Nancy, daughter of William Stanley. He owned the house built on a part of the land formerly owned by Benjamin Stinson, where he always resided. He died very suddenly; he retired in his usual health, and in the morning was found dead in bed. His death occurred in 1894, aged sixty-seven years. His wife died in 1866, at the age of thirty-five years.

Thomas Dunbar.

Thomas Dunbar came here in 1819 when a child eight years old, and was brought up in the family of Benjamin Smith. His parents resided at Deer Isle, where he had a brother Elisha, who died in 1893, at the age of seventy-five years. Thomas married Susan, a daughter of David Smith, 2d; he separated from his wife, after which he spent a roving life. After the marriage of his son, he went to Ellsworth to live with him, and died there, about eighty years of age.

Mrs. Dunbar afterwards married a Mr. Smith, of Jonesport, and after his death she became the wife of Peter Stanley. By her first marriage Mrs. Dunbar had one child, Joseph. He married Clara Batchelder, a daughter of Rev. Theophilus Batchelder, a Baptist clergyman. She was a most excellent woman, well educated and refined, and was well known throughout Hancock county, together with her sister, Annie O. Batchelder, as an excellent school teacher. They were often selected where strict discipline was required; they were large, muscular women and capable of meeting any emergency that might arise in school.

After the death of her husband Mrs. Dunbar became the wife of Daniel S. Beal, a wealthy man of Ellsworth. He was at the time of this marriage about eighty years of age, and had a family by his first wife. After his death, which occurred a few months after his marriage, it was found that he had willed his property to his second wife; his children contested the will, and, after a long trial which attracted a great deal of attention, the will was broken. Mrs. Beal died in Ellsworth in 1893.

William Nutter.

William Nutter came here about the year 1800 from Mount Desert, and was a brother of Alexander Nutter, whom we have noticed as being the first settler at Irish point. He came soon after the departure of Joseph Prince, and took up all the land south of where Parker Bridges now owns, to the salt water. He built a small house where Rodney Sadler's now stands, he at that time being the only inhabitant on that side of the harbor. His wife was Amy Rich, of Mount Desert. Mr. Nutter died in Portland while there in a vessel. They were the parents of five children — one daughter and four sons. The daughter, Elizabeth, married Elwell W. Freethy, and now resides in Brooklin. Benjamin, the oldest son, married Eliza, a daughter of Eben Herrick; James and William were lost at sea; Josiah married Judith Roberts, and settled in Brooklin.

After the death of her husband, Mrs. Nutter married Eben Herrick, of Brooklin; she sold her place here and removed to Brooklin, where she spent the remainder of her life. By Mr. Herrick she had two children — Emma and Alethia, both of whom married in Boston. Mrs. Herrick died in 1866.

Joshua Sadler.

Joshua Sadler came here in 1834, and his two brothers, Thomas and Moses, came about two years later. The Sadler family came to Maine from Gloucester. They settled in Georgetown, where these three brothers were born.

Joshua married Mary Crabtree, of Vinalhaven, where they lived for several years, a part of their children having been born there. When he came to this island he bought the land now owned by Rodney Sadler, besides the large tract extending to the south and southwest of this place to the salt water. This he bought of the widow of William Nutter, who was the first settler on this land. Mr. Nutter had built a small house where Rodney Sadler's now stands. After Thomas came the two brothers, and lived for some time in this small house. They afterwards divided the tract of land that Joshua had taken up, the latter taking the southern half including the "Point", and Thomas had the northern half. Joshua then built a house where Mrs. Margaret Sprague now lives. They were the parents of fourteen children.

Mr. Sadler sold his place — the southern part to John Ross, and the "Point" to Silas Hardy. He then went to Ellsworth, where he died about the year 1864. His wife died at Deer Isle, where she went to live with her son James. Their sons were: Chaney, who married Abigail Bridges; they lived here some years, then removed to Ellsworth, where he now resides; James, who married Margaret Stinson, of Deer Isle, where he settled; George, who also lives at Deer Isle; he has been twice married: his first wife was Lydia Ball; Benjamin, who married Justina Bridges; they removed to Ellsworth; Eben, who married Lizzie Billings, of Deer Isle; he was lost at sea; after his death Mrs. Sadler became the wife of Angus McDonald; John, who died in the South while in the service of the government during the Civil war.

The daughters were: Julia, wife of Thomas Trundy, of Deer Isle; Lydia, wife of Leander Milliken, of Ellsworth; he was lost at sea: Georgiana and Betsey, who were married after they went to Ellsworth. The other children died while young.

Thomas Sadler.

Thomas Sadler, a brother of the subject of the last sketch, was born in Georgetown. As already stated, he took the northern half of the tract of land first taken up by Joshua. He built a house near where Merrill Sadler now lives. Just previous to his death he built the house now owned by Rodney C. Sadler. In 1827 he married Hannah Hunt, of Georgetown, where they spent the first eight years of their married life. At the solicitation of his brother Joshua, he came here to live. The two brothers owned a fishing vessel, and came here on account of the convenience for carrying on their business.

Mrs. Sadler, who still survives, is in her eighty-ninth year, and possesses a remarkable memory for one of her age. She related to me much concerning the early settlers here. The land they occupied was covered with alders and a young growth of spruce when she came. This land had previously been chopped over, the logs having been sawed at the mill. There were then only three or four log huts in what is now school district No. 4, none of which could be seen from her house. There were no roads, only paths through the woods. The only inhabitants besides her husband and two brothers were the widow Rebecca Sprague, two Gott brothers, John and Joseph, and on the other side of the harbor there were John Gott, sr., father of the last two named, Edward Gott, Benjamin Stinson and William Stanley. There was then no store on the island, and most of their supplies came from Rockland; these were got in exchange for wood and fish. Amid these privations and desolation their family was reared. A large family, with the large amount of work which it brings, kept them busy, and Mrs. Sadler says she was never discontented with her lot. They were the parents of eight children.

The sons were: William, who married Maria Ross and lives in Rockland; Thomas, who married Lovina Joyce; after her death he married Mrs. Julia Oakes, of Gloucester, and after her death, married Mrs. Abbie Dyer, of Vinalhaven; his home is now in Everett, Mass.; Rodney C., who married Ann Stewart, and lives on the homestead lot.

The daughters were: Clara, wife of Newell Smith; they lived in Rockland; Mr. Smith died of yellow fever in 1882; after his death Mrs. Smith married Horton Burpee; Izetta, wife of Cornelius Wasgatt; they now reside in Everett; Mary, wife of Eben Smith; he was lost at sea; she then became the wife of David H. Sprague; Elizabeth, wife of Freeland H. Benson; they reside in Seattle, Wash.; Rosilla, wife of Elias Sprague. Thomas Sadler, sr., died in 1868, aged sixty-one years.

Moses Sadler.

Moses Sadler took up the lot south of the Gott's, extending to the lot owned by his brother Thomas, which land is now owned in part by Parker Bridges' heirs. He built a house where Mr. Bridges' now stands. His wife was Eunice Smith, who died in 1863, at the age of forty-three years. Their children were: Sylvanus, who married in the South, and now resides in Seattle; Lorenzo, who was lost at sea; two children who died young.

Mr. Sadler, sr., left here and settled near the Mooseabec river. After the death of his wife he married a Mrs. Dunbar.

James T. Sprague.

James T. Sprague came here in 1820 from Union, Maine, and settled on Harbor island where he built a log house. Here he brought his family. He remained there, however, only a few years, when he went to Marshall's island. He occupied one part of the island, and Jephtha Benson had the other. Afterwards he came back and took up one hundred acres of land in the southeastern part of the island, this being a part of the lot of five hundred acres which had for many years been taxed to Michael O'Maley, and who had now ceased to own it for non-payment of taxes thereon. He built a house near the head of the long cove just below where Lemuel Sprague now lives.

The Sprague family came to Maine from Block Island and settled in the town of Union, where many of that name still reside. Mr. Spragne's father, John Sprague, had a family of fourteen children, most of whom removed from the place of their birth.

James, the subject of this sketch, lived in Union until after he was married and had a family of three children, the present James Sprague being two years old when they came here. Mr. Sprague married Rebecca Hewes, of St. George. She had been previously married to Israel Elwell, of St. George, by whom she had two children— Israel Elwell and Susan Elwell. By Mr. Sprague she had six children—Jeremiah, Samuel and James, who were born in Union, and Eunice, John and David, born here. Mrs. Sprague died in 1862, aged seventy-nine years. The children will be further noticed.

Jeremiah Sprague married in New London, where he resided until his death.

Samuel Sprague married Phœbe Reed, of Tremont, where he settled. After the death of his wife, he married her sister, Abigail Reed. A few years previous to his death he moved here, and lived on his father's place. He died in 1854, aged forty-four years. His widow now resides at Tremont.

James Sprague took up a tract of land south of his father's, in 1838. This lot contained one hundred acres, of which he kept seventy-five acres, and the two Stanley brothers had the remaining twenty-five acres. He built the house where he still resides. He married Lois S. Morey, in 1839, by whom he had the following children, all of whom settled here: Leander, Elias, David H.,

John N., Martha and Laura. Mrs. Sprague died in 1885, aged sixty-four years.

David E. Sprague married Phœbe Smith in 1848. She was a daughter of Benjamin Smith, whose place Mr. Sprague had. It is the lot north of the carrying place. Mr. Sprague was for many years a justice of the peace, and often served as town officer. He built the house now occupied by Martin Kent. Mr. Sprague died in 1893, aged sixty-nine years. Mrs. Sprague died in 1896, aged sixty-eight years.

John N. Sprague took up the lot north of his father's; it contained one hundred acres, which he sold to Albion and Isaiah Stanley. He built the house where the latter now lives. He afterward bought the lot of land formerly owned by Joshua Sadler, now occupied by Mrs. Margaret Sprague. He lived in the house now occupied by his widow, which was built by Joshua Sadler. This land includes most of the stone quarries that are being operated at the present time by Matthew Baird, of New York. In 1843 he married Martha, daughter of William Reed, of Mt. Desert. She died in 1854, aged thirty-four years. He afterwards married Margaret Stanley, who survives him.

Eunice, the only daughter of Mr. and Mrs. James T. Sprague, became the wife of Joseph Gott.

William Stanley.

William Stanley came here from Tremont in which town he was born in 1795. His wife was Ruth, daughter of Peter Gott. They were married before coming to this place, which was about the year 1814. They moved upon the place then owned by Peter Gott, and with whom Mr. Gott lived. This lot of land adjoins on the south the lot first taken up by Moses Staples; it is now occupied by Mr. Stanley's descendants, and extends from where David Smith, 3d, now lives to Hocomock head. Their house was located where the widow of Isaiah L. Stanley now lives.

For many years Mr. Stanley was a master mariner. He served efficiently in many of the town offices. He is the ancestor of all by that name on this island. They have multiplied rapidly, and often intermarried. They have been a hardy, honest, industrious family. Few of this family ever lived to any great age. They were the parents of ten children, most of whom settled here. Mr. Stanley died in 1856, aged sixty-one years. His wife died four years previous, at the age of fifty-four years.

Their children were: Edmond, born in 1815; Joseph, Clarissa, widow of Capt. Daniel Bridges; Peter; Herbert, who died young; Nancy, wife of Hiram Kent; William, who died at the age of twenty-four years; Lucy, wife of Moses Bridges, 2d; after his death she became the wife of Freeman Gross; Mrs. Gross died in 1895, aged fifty-nine years; Isaiah L. and Freeman. The last-named and Mrs. Bridges are the only survivors of the family. The sons who lived here will be further noticed.

Edmond Stanley, together with his brother Joseph, took up the twenty-five acres of land lying southwest of James Sprague's, and which was a part of his one-hundred acre lot. His wife was Betsy, daughter of David Smith, 2d, by whom he had ten children. They were: Albion, Isaiah, Jeremiah, George, David, John, Margaret, wife of John N. Sprague, Sultana, wife of Fred Dunham, Ellen, who died unmarried, and Hannah, wife of Samuel Stanley.

Joseph Stanley settled on a lot next to his brother Edmond. His wife was Abigail Smith, sister of the wife of the subject of the last sketch. They were parents of ten children, as follows: Joseph, Horace, Ansel, Samuel, Albert, who fell from a bluff and was drowned at the age of two years; Thomas, Elizabeth, wife of Albion Stanley; Eunice, wife of Elmer Holbrook; Lucy A., wife of Stephen Dunham, jr.; Margaret, wife of George E. Trask, and Lois.

Peter Stanley lived on the place taken up by David Smith, 2d, and in whose family Mrs. Smith lived during the latter part of her life. His wife was Sarah Rice, of Long Island, by whom he had three children—Lucy A., wife of Isaiah W. Stanley; Elmira, wife of Warren Sprague; George E. After the death of his wife he married Emily Rich, of Long Island, by whom he had two children—Alwilda, wife of John Stanley, and Sarah, who married Harry Sargent, of Ellsworth, where she now resides. After the death of his second wife Peter Stanley married Mrs. Susan Smith, daughter of David Smith, 2d. Mrs. Smith had twice before been married; her first husband was Thomas Dunbar, by whom she had one child— Joseph; she afterwards married a Mr. Smith of Jonesport, by whom she had one daughter — Melissa, who married Joseph Stanley, 2d. Mrs. Stanley died in 1896, aged seventy-two years. Peter Stanley died in 1884, aged sixty-two years.

Isaiah L. Stanley lived on the place that his father settled on. His wife was Sapphira Herrick, daughter of Kimball Herrick. Mr. Stanley died in 1892, aged sixty-five years.

William Fife.

William Fife came here from New Hampshire, and built a house and store just below where Elmer Holbrook now lives. Here he carried on quite an extensive business. He seems to have been an enterprising business man, and often served as town officer. His wife was Ruth Gott, by whom he had four children. They were: Sarah J., born in 1834, who was *non compos mentis;* Elmira, born in 1836, who became the wife of Morris Rich, of Tremont; William, born in 1839; Elnathan, born in 1841. The former of the two sons is dead; the latter went to New Hampshire. His wife died in 1844, at the age of twenty-eight years. In 1845 he married Sarah Sellers, of Deer Isle. She was a daughter of William Sellers, who came to Deer Isle from York, Maine, in 1775. His wife soon separated from him, and he moved to Ellsworth where he died in 1855. In 1862 Mrs. Fife married Charles Fish, of Thorndike. She died two years later in Union, at the age of fifty-six years.

Jephtha Benson.

Jephtha Benson was born in Oxford county, Maine, near 1757, and was said to have been married there, but of this first family we have no record. While a young man he entered the Revolutionary war and served throughout the war. In the year 1800 he came to Little Deer Isle, and took up a tract of land. This afterwards became the property of Silas L. Hardy, by whom it was occupied until his death in 1859. It is now the property of Mr. Hardy's sons.

Mr. Benson again entered the service of the government at the breaking out of the war of 1812. He was at Bagaduce when the British took possession of that town. He had in his possession an old English rifle which he got at Castine at this time; it was highly prized by him, and he kept it until his death.

At the close of the war of 1812 he went to Marshall's island, which lies to the west of Swan's Island. It is a very valuable island to this day, being assessed at $10,000 by the State, and was, as we have seen, included in Swan's purchase. This island Mr. Benson leased to Swan's agent. He was the first settler there. He cleared the land and built a log house. Afterwards he built a timber house which has long since gone to decay.

He married Mrs. Mary Ross, widow of John Ross, who lived in Brunswick. She was a daughter of Thomas Kench, whom we have noticed as being the first settler in this town. Mr. Ross's father, Barton Ross, was a pioneer settler of Brunswick, and owned a large tract of land there. At his death he divided his property among his six children, one of whom was John Ross, whom we have mentioned. He built a house upon his lot, and reared his family. He sailed in a ship from Castine, at which place he married his wife, Mary Kench. Mr. Ross was lost at sea in 1817, while engaged in the West India trade. They had three children, whom Mrs. Ross brought to Marshall's island when she married Mr. Benson. These children were: John, born in 1812, Thomas, and a daughter Evelyn, who died unmarried. The children of Mr. and Mrs. Benson were: Sarah, who married and lives in Charlestown, Mass.; Mary, who became the wife of Edwin Smith, and resided at Jamaica Plain; Maria, who married a Mr. Wood, of Boston; Jephtha and Judson, who were lost at sea; Freelan H., the only surviving son, lives at Seattle, Wash. When Mr. Benson came to Marshall's island he only leased the property, so he secured no title to it by his long residence there. He was dispossessed by Rufus B. Allyn, Swan's agent, in 1835, after which he removed to Brooksville, where he died at the age of ninety-eight years. After his death Mrs. Benson came to Swan's Island and resided with her children until her death, which occurred in 1874, at the age of eighty-two years. Marshall's island was afterwards sold to John B. Redman, of Brooksville, and Charles K. Tilden, of Castine. It is at present owned by Oliver Lane, of Brooklin.

John Ross was born at Brunswick, and came with his mother to Marshall's island. His wife was Elizabeth, a daughter of Moses Bridges. They lived for some years on

Calf island. He then bought a piece of land of Benjamin Stinson, and built the house where Hezekiah Holbrook now lives. Mr. Ross died in 1845, aged twenty-nine years. Their children were Julia, Evelyn, Emma, and some others who died young. Mrs. Ross, in 1848, married William Annis, who was born in Appleton in 1802. They resided here until 1855, when they removed to Deer Isle and bought the place near Stinson's Neck bar. They were the parents of several children who still reside at Deer Isle. Mr. Annis was drowned in February, 1872, while crossing the bar near his home. He was seventy years of age. Mrs. Annis was born in Sedgwick in 1818, and died at Deer Isle December 19, 1892.

Thomas Ross was born in Brunswick, and for several years after his mother married Jephtha Benson, he lived with his grandfather, Thomas Kench, at Brooksville. He is the only survivor of the family, and resides in Malden, Mass. His wife was Diana Norwood, of Mount Desert. He bought one acre of land of Silas Hardy, and in 1845 built the house which is standing near the shore below Hiram Stanley's house. When Joshua Sadler moved away, Mr. Ross bought all of his possessions — about one hundred acres, which includes all the land south of the road leading from No. 4 school-house to the point. In 1860 he sold his property here, and removed to Addison, where he bought a farm. Their children were: John, who married Fannie Wass, of Addison; he died of yellow fever while captain of a brig bound for San Domingo; they put in at Fortune Island, where he died and was buried;

Mary, wife of Oscar Evans, of Boston; Sarah, wife of George Haskell, of Boston; Ella and Malinda, who died young; Charles, who was lost at sea; Lizzie, wife of Sampson Hewson; Laura, wife of Frank Hickson. The last two reside at Malden, Mass., and are the only surviving children. Mr. Ross at present resides in this town.

Silas Hardy.

Silas Hardy came here in 1825, and bought Harbor island of Seth and Zachariah Kempton when they left this place. He was a son of Capt. Peter Hardy, jr., of Deer Isle, whose ancestors came to Deer Isle from Worcester, Mass. Mr. Hardy married Hannah Adams, a sister of John Adams, of Beverly. He traded for a few years in a store on Harbor island where Kempton Brothers formerly traded. He sold Harbor island to William Stinson, and bought of Joshua Sadler the point of land near the site of Swan's mills. Here he built a house and store, and did a large business. It was the only store on the island at the time, and, in fact, it was the first large store on the island. Others had traded here before, but they kept only a small stock of goods, such as fishermen's supplies. As his business grew he not only secured the trade of the island population, but also did a brisk business fitting the large fleet which here found a market for its fish. He bought and cured a large amount of fish. He also did quite a business in shipbuilding; the largest vessel he built in 1835, called the "Henry M. Johnson", which he built for parties in Newark, New Jersey. Mr. Hardy was one of the first justices of the peace appointed on the island, and nearly all the marriage ceremonies in those times were performed by him. He had acquired a good education, and was an excellent business man.

They were the parents of six children — three sons and three daughters. The sons were: Silas, jr., a carpenter, who resides in the West; he is unmarried; Thompson H., who was killed in the Civil war; Arthur W., who died at the age of twenty-three years. The daughters were: Mary E., wife of Oliver Lane, of Stinson's Neck, Deer Isle; Emma and Effie J., who reside in Chicago. Mr. Hardy, sr., left here in 1847. He sold "the point" to Moses Bridges in exchange for a part of Marshall's island. This in turn he sold to Oliver Lane, the present owner. After leaving here, Mr. Hardy lived for several years at Winterport. During this time he sailed in a ship between New York and Australia. From one of these voyages he did not return, and it was supposed that he died in Australia. His wife then went to Illinois with her brother, John Adams, where she now lives at a very advanced age.

John Adams.

John Adams came here in 1840 from Beverly, Mass. His wife was Lucy, daughter of Peter Hardy, jr., of Deer Isle, and a sister of Silas Hardy, with whom Mr. Adams came to work when Mr. Hardy began trading. He was a carpenter and worked at his business here and at Deer Isle. He afterward went to Winterport, and later removed to Illinois. Mr. Adams was well educated, and for a number of years taught school here, and often served as town officer. He died in 1885.

They were the parents of six children, as follows: Thomas J., who was a soldier in the Civil war; after the war he bought an orange grove in Florida; he now resides in Indian territory; Lucy J., who was a school teacher in the West; she was drowned while boating on Chrystal lake, Illinois; Ellen, who is a teacher; Mary A. and Zella, who are unmarried and reside in the West; Lulu, who died at the age of two years.

HARBOR ISLAND.

Harbor island forms the southern side to Old Harbor, and contains one hundred and forty-four acres. This seems to have been an attractive location for the earliest settlers, as many made this temporarily their home. It was first settled, as has been recorded, by Thomas Kench, near the year 1777. After Swan's purchase this island came into the possession of Joseph Prince, of Beverly, who remained until about the year 1800. In 1791 David Smith settled on this island, and while here Sarah, his daughter, was born in the year 1792, being the first white child born on this island. It afterwards became the property of Col. Henry Jackson, of Boston. He, however, probably never considered it as valuable property, and soon other settlers took possession of it. Dr. Thurston and a Mr. Bunker lived here for some years at an early date. Here they kept a small store of general merchandise. The other settlers will be noticed more in detail.

Zachariah Kempton.

Zachariah Kempton came to Harbor island from Hampden, Maine, in 1821, and staid about four years. He, together with his brother, who came at the same time, built a house and store on Harbor island, and did considerable trading. They bought and cured fish and fitted out vessels. He soon brought his family here. His wife was Mary Evans, and they were the parents of five children — Frank, David, Zachariah, William and Jane. These children are all dead except Zachariah and William, who reside in Brooklyn, N. Y. Mr. Kempton was a carpenter; he learned his trade of his father, who was a shipbuilder and one of the pioneer settlers of Frankfort. This Kempton family came to Frankfort from Plymouth, Mass., where they settled when they came from England. No member of this family is now living in New England except a niece of the subject of this sketch; she is the wife of Alfred H. Slatten, of Hampden Corner, Maine. Mr. Kempton died in 1844.

Seth Kempton.

Seth Kempton came with his brother Zachariah to Harbor island. He was a young man and unmarried. When he left this place in 1825 he settled in Hampden. His wife was Lucy Brown, of Orrington, by whom he had seven children — Seth, Zachariah, Harvey, Joseph, Lucy, Lucinda and Eliza. Joseph settled in Colorado, Eliza and Harvey in Iowa, whence Mr. Kempton's whole family moved in 1839. The other children settled in the western states, and none of them ever returned to the place of their birth. Mr. Kempton died in six weeks after his arrival in Iowa. The property on Harbor island belonging to the Kempton brothers was bought by Silas Hardy. After trading there a few years this property came into the possession of William Stinson. Hardy and Oliver Lane, Mr. Stinson's heirs, now own it.

Hardy Lane.

Hardy Lane came here from Deer Isle near the year 1835. He was the son of Oliver Lane, sr., and was born in 1820. He, with his brother Oliver, bought Harbor island of Silas Hardy. His wife was Livonia Stinson, by whom he had nine children. They were: Hannah, Sarah, Livonia, who settled at Deer Isle; Oliver, jr., who resides in Chicago; Silas, who bought a large farm where he now resides at West Gardiner; William, who lives in Seattle, Wash.; Mary and Amasa, who are in Brooklyn, N. Y.; Lizzie, who lives in Brockton, Mass. Mr. Lane returned to Deer Isle in 1861. Mr. Lane was a candidate for representative to the legislature at Deer Isle in 1873. He received fifty-four votes to one hundred and eleven for William Babbidge. He died in 1886, aged sixty-six years.

Oliver Lane.

Oliver Lane was born at Deer Isle in 1822, and, as before stated, bought Harbor island with his brother Hardy in 1835. The two families lived together for some years, when Oliver sold his part to William Stinson, whose wife,

Elizabeth Lane, was an only sister of the subject of this sketch. Mr. Lane afterwards bought Marshall island. The former owner had been Swan, during whose ownership it was occupied by Jephtha Benson, later by Moses Bridges and Silas Hardy. About this time it came into the possession of Charles K. Tilden, of Castine, and Erastus Redman, of Brooksville, by whom it was mortgaged to Boston parties. Mr. Lane bought it of these parties at an excellent trade, as the island is quite valuable, being assessed at about $10,000. Mr. Lane resided here until 1874, when he went to Sedgwick, where he now resides. His wife was Keturah Stinson, by whom he had five children — Hardy, Fred, Georgie, Vesta and John.

Robert Mitchell.

Robert Mitchell was born in Dublin, Ireland, March 28, 1790, and came to this country as an emigrant in 1814. After a long, tedious voyage of six weeks, they saw land through the fog, and anchored in Old Harbor. It was one of the old-fashioned emigrant ships, a poor sailer, and furnished still poorer accommodations to its passengers. There were three hundred and sixty emigrants aboard, most of whom were Irish. It was Sunday morning when they anchored. Many of the emigrants came ashore, some of whom were invited to attend a religious service held at the house of David Smith at the " north ". While here they learned that one of their countrymen, John Finney, lived on the eastern side of the island, and a large number of them went across the island to pay Mr. Finney a visit, and stayed with him over night. Mr. Finney's small house made it inconvenient for him to accommodate so large a company, but he was equal to the emergency. He had recently sheared his sheep, the wool of which he spread upon the floor, thus making a comfortable bed for them all.

Mr. Mitchell alone remained; the others returned to the ship, which sailed the next morning for Portland. Mr. Mitchell never heard from any of the company afterwards. He was hired by Abel Staples, with whom he worked two years. In 1820 he married Mr. Staples' daughter, Judith. He bought land on Placentia, and went there to live. There was a log house on the island, and in this they began housekeeping. This island was then covered with a dense forest, much of which he cut off and sold. The land thus cleared made an excellent farm. In three years he had built a frame house. They had a family of nine children, three of whom died young. Mr. Mitchell was an active member of the Methodist church. He died in 1861, aged seventy-one years. Mrs. Mitchell died twenty years earlier, aged forty-four years. The following are notices of their children:

George W. was born in 1822, and married Almira Stanley, a daughter of Joseph Stanley, of Steuben. He was for many years a sea captain. After a long voyage he arrived at Boston where he met a terrible death. He was walking on a railroad track when his foot caught in a frog, and to his consternation he saw a train approaching. He tried in vain to extricate himself, but finding it useless, he leaned as far back as he could in hopes of saving his life by losing his leg. But just then a train came rushing in the opposite direction; he was struck, thrown high into the air, and came down crushed and lifeless. The Masons, of which order he was a member, sent his body home to Calais, where he was buried in April, 1879. He left a widow and three children. The widow and one child now reside in Calais.

Jane A. was born at Swan's Island in 1824. She married Benjamin Murphy, of Tremont, where she has always resided. Mr. Murphy died in 1886, leaving his widow with eight children. Mrs. Murphy, until her death, resided with her youngest daughter at Bass Harbor. She died in 1898, aged seventy-four years.

Sarah B. was born at Swan's Island in 1826. She became the wife of Adam Reed, of Tremont. For many years he was a successful master mariner. He followed the sea until near the close of his life, when, on account of failing health, he was obliged to abandon it. He died in Jacksonville, Florida, where he had gone for his health. Mrs. Reed at present resides in Oakland, Mass.

Judith S. died at the age of seven years.

Marietta B. was born at Placentia in 1836. She was the wife of Charles Mitchell, of Bass Harbor. Mrs. Mitchell died very suddenly in 1872, at the age of thirty-eight years.

Robert, jr., was born at Placentia in 1836. He married Mary J. Ober, of Tremont. He followed the sea and was mate of a New York vessel at the time of his death. They were anchored off Ricker's Island. The night was bright moonlight, yet a watch was kept on deck. Mr. Mitchell's watch expired at 3 a. m.; he went below into the cabin, called the captain, told him it was his watch, and then retired. The captain, only partially aroused, fell asleep again. While they slept a "river pirate" came aboard the vessel. He proceeded at once to the captain's berth, placed a revolver at his ear, and told him if he uttered a sound he would blow his brains out. The robber secured a watch, $39 in cash, and such other articles as he could readily obtain. He then backed out of the cabin, still keeping the captain covered with his revolver. The captain then whispered to Mitchell that a robber was aboard, when Mitchell came out of his berth, probably half asleep, and started up the steps behind the robber, who turned around and fired, the ball passing through Mitchell's body and into the deck. He never spoke, and died in a few minutes. His body was buried in New York. This happened in 1865, at the age of twenty-nine years.

Joshua S. Trask.

Joshua S. Trask came here from Stillwater, Maine, about the year 1825, and married Mary Staples. He then went to Long Island where he traded for several years, doing quite a business. Although the island was small and the inhabitants few, yet this was a resort for many fishing vessels, it being near the fishing grounds, and furnished a good harbor. It was from these vessels principally that he received his custom. He afterwards came here and settled near the end of the point of land formerly owned by Washington Staples, now called Trask's point, where he built a house. He was a man of liberal education, and possessed a wonderful memory. His favorite study was history, French history being his favorite. He was a great admirer of Napoleon, after whom he named one of his sons. For several years he taught school here with good success. He was an active man in town affairs, and for many years was justice of the peace.

They were the parents of eleven children. Mr. Trask was lost in the Bay of Chaleur during the great gale of Oct. 3, 1851. He was in the schooner "Henry Clay", commanded by John Walls. The vessel foundered in the gale and all hands were lost. His age was forty-four years. Mrs. Trask afterwards became the wife of Philip Moore, of Gott's Island, by whom she had three children, none of whom reached adult age. Mrs. Moore is now dead.

The sons of Mr. and Mrs. Trask were: Capt. Orlando, who married the widow of Byron Joyce, and lives near where his father settled; Napoleon B., who married Cynthia Staples; he died at Sydney, C. B., in 1865, aged twenty-nine years; Lorenzo S., who lives at Tremont. The daughters were: Lucinda, wife of Enoch Moore, of Gott's Island; Flavilla, wife of George Moore, of Tremont: Elmira; several other children died in infancy.

Jacob S. Reed.

Jacob S. Reed came here from Brooklin in 1845, and bought nine acres of land from the Joyce lot, which at this time was owned by William Joyce. Some years previous to his coming here he bought a small part of the lot of land he afterwards occupied, through which ran a large stream of water. This he dammed and it proved to be an excellent mill privilege. This was the place where Prince wished to locate a mill. Mr. Reed took down a mill which he had been running in Brooklin, and erected it over this stream. While at Brooklin his gristmill was first operated by wind, and later by horse-power. This was a rather expensive mode of manufacture, so he came here where he might utilize this water privilege. At this time a greater part of the bread was made from the flour of corn and barley which were raised on the island. William Joyce operated the mill several years; afterwards Mr. Reed came himself, bought more land and built a house, which is still known as the Reed house. Soon after this time manufactured wheat flour became cheaper, so less grain was raised here, and after a short time the mill was closed.

Mr. Reed was a man of marked individuality and sterling integrity. He was three times married. His first wife was Sarah, daughter of Moses Staples, 2d; she died in 1865, aged fifty-nine years; his second wife was Mary Harding, of Boston, who died in 1871, aged thirty-nine years; his third wife was Isabel S. Joyce, who died in 1888, aged sixty-eight years. Mr. Reed died in Scarboro where he went to live with his children. His death occurred in 1888, at the age of eighty-four years.

The following were his children: Allen G. and Lemuel, who live in Scarboro; Simeon S. and Joseph;

Emily, wife of Daniel H. Babbidge; he was lost in the schooner "Constitution" off Nausett light, Cape Cod, in 1860, at the age of twenty-eight years; after his death she married Winthrop B. Lane, of Deer Isle: Mrs. Lane was in the schooner "S. J. Collins" that was lost at sea in 1867, together with her two daughters, Lillian, aged eight years, and Grace, aged one year; Susan, wife of Ezra Torrey; he was drowned in 1865; Mary E., wife of Nelson Stinson; they now reside in Harpswell; Sarah A. and Myra, who died young.

Abram Holbrook.

Abram Holbrook came from Deer Isle in 1836, and settled here on the place owned by Samuel Kent, and afterwards lived for a number of years on Buckle island. He never owned any property here. Later he returned to Deer Isle, and lived the remainder of his life at Webb's cove in that town. He was over seventy years of age at his death. His wife was Martha Morey, a sister of Elias Morey, jr., whom we have noticed. They were the parents of eight children, as follows: Abram, jr., who married Abbie Herrick; Hezekiah, who married Angelina Smith; after her death he married Parthanea Gott; these two sons reside here at present; Mary A., wife of Amos C. Beal, of Grand Menan; Rosetta, wife of Benjamin Harvey, of Deer Isle; Susan, Henry, John and an infant died young.

Mr. Holbrook's father, Elisha Holbrook, came from Cape Cod and settled at Isle au Haut about the year 1800.

There he married a daughter of Abiathar Smith. His children were: Abram, the subject of this sketch; Simon, who went away from home when a young man; Daniel, who lived at Vinal Haven; he was killed by falling from a derrick used in hoisting stone, up which he had gone for the purpose of fixing a tackle; the daughters were the wives of Joseph Morey and afterwards Humphrey Webster; of Samuel Black, and of a Mr. Hall who lived near Belfast; another daughter was reared in the family of Capt. Samuel Turner.

Alexander Kiff.

Alexander Kiff came here from St. George, Maine, in 1841, and lived in a house south of where Parker Bridges now resides. He married, in 1823, Susan Robinson Gilchrist, of St. George, at which place they lived for several years. They moved to Gloucester in 1849. Mr. Kiff died there in 1883, aged eighty-two years; his wife died in 1891, aged eighty-seven years.

They were the parents of the following children: Eliza, born in 1827, who was the first wife of Seth Stockbridge; she died in 1865, aged thirty-eight years; Clarissa, who is the wife of Eben Stockbridge; they reside in Gloucester; William, who married, in 1853, Frances Tibbetts; Nancy, who was the wife of David Elwell: after his death she became the second wife of Seth Stockbridge; she died in 1884, aged forty-seven years.

Israel Conary.

Israel Conary came here in 1820, and settled on a lot of land known as "City point". His wife was Martha Gott. He afterwards moved to Black or Conary's island, where he lived some years; later he came back to this town and bought a part of the lot then owned by Joseph Gott; he built the house where David Stanley now resides. After having reared their family here they moved to Bluehill, where Mr. and Mrs. Conary died.

They were the parents of the following children: Moses, who married Mary A. Smith, a daughter of David Smith. 2d; John, who was lost at sea; William, who died unmarried; Nancy, who was the wife of Hezekiah Morey; she is the only one of the family now residing here; Amaziah, who married Maria Malcolm, of Newcastle; Emma, who was the wife of Harvey Conary, of Deer Isle; Joseph, who died unmarried at Staten Island, New York.

The ancestor of this Conary family, Thomas Conary, emigrated to this country from Ireland, and was the first settler on Conary's island in Eggemoggin reach. His first wife was a daughter of the ancestor of the Limeburner family, now living in Brooksville, by adoption. Mr. Limeburner came from Scotland before the Revolutionary war, and with him came, besides his own family, a son and a daughter adopted by him. The son, Cunningham Limeburner, died at an advanced age, not far from 1825, in Brooksville, and the daughter, Mrs. Conary, was his sister by birth. After her death he married a daughter of Mrs. Mercy Staples, and a sister of Moses Staples, sr., of this town, and by both marriages he had ten sons. Their descendants, most of whom reared large families, have settled in many towns in this section of the State.

Solomon Barbour.

Solomon Barbour came here from Deer Isle in 1843, and bought the lot of land before described as belonging to Alexander Staples. He erected the building now standing thereon, and built a store, where he traded for some years. Previous to this time he had been a successful master mariner. His wife was Harriet, daughter of Abel E. Staples. Mr. Barbour's grandfather, also Solomon Barbour, came to Deer Isle from Massachusetts in 1793. His wife was Deborah Faxon, of Braintree, who, it is said, when she was young, resided for some years in the family of John Adams, President of the United States; while with the family, John Quincy Adams was an infant, of whom she had the care.

Mr. Barbour, sr., was a baker by trade. He joined the Continental army near the beginning of the Revolutionary war and served until its close; he received a pension until his death, which occurred in 1830. After his death his widow continued to receive the pension under the act to grant pensions to the widows of Revolutionary soldiers. She died in 1852, at the age of ninety-two years.

Solomon Barbour, jr., married after coming to this town, where he continued to reside until his death in 1896, at the age of eighty-one years. His widow still occupies the homestead. They were the parents of Seth and

George Barbour, both of whom are dead, and Capt. Alvah Barbour, who at present is captain of the passenger steamer "Vinalhaven". The daughters were: Edna, wife of W. Leslie Joyce, and Cornelia, wife of Emery. E. Joyce.

Moses Bridges.

Moses Bridges came to this island in 1847. He was born in Sedgwick, March 17, 1790. Here he married Emily Eaton; they lived a few years in Sedgwick, where their oldest child was born in 1818. He bought of Rufus B. Allyn, Swan's agent, the eastern Calf island, containing one hundred and sixty-two acres, for which he paid $400. He was given a deed of the island by Allyn May 23, 1823, and a mortgage was given; this mortgage was discharged in December, 1839. He then disposed of this property and moved to Marshall's island. Whether he had any legal title to the part of the island he occupied, we do not know, but in 1847 he exchanged his part of Marshall's island with Silas Hardy for the "Point" below Sadler's. It is claimed there was a mortgage on this place when Mr. Bridges bought it and later it was foreclosed, which turned Mr. Bridges out of doors in his old age. Mr. Bridges died in 1873, aged eighty-three years; his wife died in 1850, aged fifty-four years. Mr. and Mrs. Bridges were the parents of eleven children.

The daughters were: Betsey, who became the wife of John Ross, who was drowned in 1845, aged twenty-nine years; in 1848 Mrs. Ross married William Annis;

he, also, lost his life by drowning; Mrs. Annis died in 1895, aged seventy-four years; Julia A., who married in 1843 Consider Bridges; this occurred while the Bridges family was living on Marshall's island; they settled in Bucksport; she died about 1895, aged seventy-six years; Emily, who married, in 1844, Isaac H. Keith; Abigail, who married Chaney Sadler; Jane, who was the wife of John Joyce; Justina, who was the wife of Albert Smith; the last four settled in Ellsworth; Naomi, who married Frank Wilson, of Orono.

The sons were: Daniel and Parker, who will be further noticed; Stillman, who married Caroline Pomroy; he died at this place; Moses, 2d, who married Lucy Stanley; after his death she married Freeman Gross, of Orland.

Daniel Bridges married Clarissa Stanley and bought the lot of land formerly owned by John Gott, and built the house where his son Wilmer now resides. Their children were: Edmond F., Leaman, who died in 1887, aged thirty-four; James and Wilmer; Deborah, wife of William S. Joyce; Emily, wife of Roland Stewart; Dianthia, wife of Harris J. Gott; Algia, wife of Lewis Staples. Mr. Bridges died in 1887, aged sixty-four years. His widow still survives at an advanced age.

Parker Bridges bought the lot of Moses Sadler in 1859. On this lot he built the house now occupied by his widow. His wife was Mary A., daughter of David E. Conary, of Deer Isle, whom he married in 1852. Their children were: Addison, Harvey, Reuben, who was lost at sea Dec. 18, 1883, aged twenty-four years; David, Lewis and Willard. The daughters were: Amelia F., wife of Edward E. Rankins, of Rockland; she died in 1888, aged thirty-three years; Susan, wife of Oliver Bowley.

This completes the record of the early settlers of Swan's Island. It includes all those who made their homes here for any length of time, as far as I have been able to ascertain. I have tried to make the record of each family as complete and accurate as possible. In some cases it has been impossible to trace them all, as so few records had been preserved. If some families have been noticed more in detail than others, it has been for the reason that better and more thorough records have been at my disposal.

CHAPTER V.

GOTT'S ISLAND.

It has been thought best to include in this work a notice of the early settlers of Gott's Island, as the people from that island have so often intermarried with the people of Swan's Island, and many of them have changed their residences from the one place to the other that their histories are almost inseparable.

Champlain was the first explorer who makes mention of Gott's Island, which the French then called Petit Plaisants (Little Placentia), by which name this island was called until 1789, when it was purchased by Daniel Gott, since which it has been known as Gott's Island. Champlain, while on this voyage of discovery in September, 1604, made the first map of this coast. On this map we find the French had given names to many of these islands, either at this time or previous to Champlain's visit. Many of the names given to them by the French have been retained to the present day, *e. g.*, Isle au Haut, Grand Menan, Petit Menan, Mount Desert (which means "The Isle of the Desert Mountains"), Petit Plaisants and Grand Plaisants (Little and Great Placentia) which mean, when translated, "The Little Beautiful Island" and "The Large Beautiful Island", and Brule-cote, afterwards incorrectly translated into Burnt Coat by which Swan's Island was formerly known. The French from this time had possession of the coast from the Penobscot bay to the St. Croix river. This claim was not conceded, however, by the Massachusetts Bay colony, which was jealous of the encroachment of the French. The French had established trading-posts at many places along the coast.

During the spring of 1688 Sir John Andros, of the Massachusetts Bay colony, desiring to determine the number of those stations and the strength of the French occupation, sent a whale-boat down the shore to reconnoitre and check the French advance. They found two French families — (1) at Penobscot (Castine) Baron Castine, his family and Ranne, his servant; (2) at Eggemoggin reach Charles St. Robin, his son and daughter, La Fleur and wife; (3) near Mount Desert, Little Placentia (Gott's Island), he found Lowry, wife and child who were French, and Hinds, wife and four children (English under French protection); (4) east side of Mount Desert, Winscheag bay, Cadalac and wife; (5) at St. Machias, Martell, John Breton, wife and child, of Jersey. Latter, wife and three children; (6) Passamaquoddy and St. Croix, St. Robin, wife and son Lettrell, John Minus, wife and four children, Lambert, Jolly Clive, his servant, Torza, Lena, his servant. The above enumeration is found recorded in the Massachusetts historical society, and was made May 11, 1688.

So the first account of a settlement on Gott's Island was this record. How long they had been there, or where they came from, is not known. Traces of where Hinds and Lowry lived are still to be seen, one of which is in Charles Welch's field, and another near by in Samuel Gott's field. A thorn tree still grows near where each one of these houses was located, which is supposed to have been planted by these families, as they were found growing there when Daniel Gott came to the island in 1789. The thorn tree in Mr. Welch's field is but a few rods from the shore, and the traces of where the house stood are pretty well obliterated. The thorn bush in Mr. Gott's field stands at what is called the fore shore bank. This bank, which is made up mostly of clam shells, has been gradually washed away by the action of the sea, so that only a part of the cellar over which one of these settlers lived is visible; the rest is washed away, and the thorn tree now is partly over the bank.

The Massachusetts Bay colony, in May, 1704, sent out an expedition under Capt. Church against the French and Indians along the coast. The French trading posts were broken up, and many of the settlers were taken prisoners; this may have been the fate of Hinds and Lowry. I do not find any further record of settlers on Little Placentia until some eighty years later, when it became the property of Mr. Gott. It is probable that this island was the temporary abode of fishermen during a greater part of the interval between the departure of Hinds and Lowry and the arrival of Mr. Gott; but if such there were, no records of them have been preserved.

The Gott family which first settled at Mount Desert came from Gloucester, Mass. They had very large families, and were a vigorous, hardy race; most of their large families of descendants reached adult age, married, very often, among their own relations, they in turn having large families. So they have spread far and wide, and they and their descendants form a large proportion of the inhabitants in all the towns surrounding their early settlement. They are especially numerous at Mount Desert, Gott's Island, Swan's Island and Deer Isle. On account of their frequently marrying people of their own name, and the frequent repetition of names in the different branches of this family, their genealogy is confusing.

Charles Gott, the ancestor of the Gott family in America, came to this country in 1628, and was of the company that came over with John Endicott, afterwards governor. This company sailed from Weymouth, England, June 20, 1628, and arrived at Salem on Sept. 6, of the same year.

Daniel Gott, of Gloucester, had a large and interesting family. Several of his children came to the towns mentioned above. A part only settled on the island under consideration, but their families are so connected that their record will be given here. Three of his daughters married three brothers, Richardson by name: (1) Elizabeth married Stephen Richardson, of Gloucester, and settled at West Bass Harbor, over an old cellar in the field back of Jacob Sawyer's present residence; (2) Margaret married Thomas Richardson, of Gloucester, and settled at East Bass Harbor, over a cellar about half way between the store and present residence of Perry W. Richardson; (3)

Rachel married James Richardson, of Gloucester, and settled at Somesville about the time that Abraham Somes made the first permanent settlement in 1762 or '63. In August, 1763, George Richardson was born, he being the first child born to white parents on Mount Desert.

Another daughter of Daniel Gott, of Gloucester, named Eunice, married Capt. Benjamin Stockbridge, of Gloucester; they had one son, Benjamin, jr., who settled at Deer Isle. After the husband died Mrs. Stockbridge became the wife of Capt. John Thurston, of Gloucester. By this second marriage their children were: Ambrose, who married Polly Gamage; Amos, who married Mary Gott; Stephen married Mrs. Pierce Carter; William married Nancy Foster; John, jr., who married Sarah Foster. All these were born in Gloucester. Then about 1784, Capt. Thurston moved his growing family and his stepson, Benjamin Stockbridge, to Deer Isle, where the following children were born: Solomon, who married Sarah Gott; Lois, who was the wife of a Mr. Hooper; after his death she married Charles Gott, her cousin; Eunice, who was the wife of David Smith, of Swan's Island; Susan, who was the first wife of Charles Gott. So the Thurston and Stockbridge families of Deer Isle were closely related to the Gotts, of Gott's Island. Most of these children's families have been considered more in detail elsewhere in this book.

Daniel Gott, of Gloucester, also had two sons—Daniel, whom we shall notice as the original purchaser of Gott's Island, and William. Peter Gott, whom we have recorded as having settled and reared his family on Swan's Island, was a cousin to this family.

William Gott, a son of Daniel Gott, of Gloucester, married Patience Richardson, and settled at Mason's point (Somesville) about 1776 or 1778. He died soon after, when his widow married Andrew Tarr and settled at Fernald's point (Southwest Harbor). By her first marriage Mrs. Gott's children were: Elial, who was never married; he was killed in a drunken fray in 1790; Rachel, who married a Mr. York; they had no children; after Mr. York's death she became the wife of a Mr. Dean; they had one child, Rhoda, who died young. By her second marriage her children were: Comfort, who married Tobias Fernald, of Kittery, Maine; Andrew, jr., married, in 1795, Esther Stanwood; Daniel, who married, in 1799, Tryphosia Hudlock.

(1) Comfort and Tobias Fernald's children were: Daniel, born in 1808, was never married; is living (1894); Eben, born in 1810, married Sophronia Wasgatt. (The above were the parents of Rev. O. H. Fernald.)

(2) Andrew Tarr, jr., married Esther Stanwood. They had one son, also Andrew Tarr, born in 1796.

(3) Daniel Tarr married Tryphosia Hudlock. Their children were: Daniel, Jonathan H., Samuel H., of whom there is no record. Another son, Aaron, walked overboard in his sleep from the steamer "Royal Tar"; Sarah married a Mr. Stephens.

Daniel Gott, a son of Daniel Gott, of Gloucester, first settled at Norwood's Cove, Tremont, some time previous to the Revolutionary war. His wife was Hannah Norwood. Here, in 1777, their first child was born. Soon after this, Mr. Gott moved to Gott's Island, it receiving its name from him; previous to this time it was called Little Placentia island. He afterwards bought this island of the commonwealth of Massachusetts, in consideration of the sum of £18. His deed was dated March 25, 1789, and is still in a good state of preservation; it is in the hands of Mr. Gott's descendants; he thus became, as far as we have any record, the first owner of the island. The two Bass Harbor residences of the sisters and the Gott's Island residence were in full view.

These families, after settling here, had hard work to support their families, depending almost solely upon the fishing business, and being so far away from any place where supplies could be obtained. An incident of great trial in the family of the Gotts and Richardsons occurred at Bass Harbor. They were short of provisions. Late in the fall of 1765 (or thereabout) they sent a load of staves to Gloucester to be exchanged for provisions to last them through the winter. When the provisions arrived they were stored at Thomas Richardson's, East Bass Harbor. That night Mr. Richardson and wife, having put their two children, Thomas, jr., and Puah, in bed, they harnessed an ox single and started for Beech Hill by moonlight, following a wood track one mile east, and then along an Indian trail seven or eight miles to Beech Hill and Somesville to notify them that provisions had arrived. On their return near midnight, when at the top of Beech Hill mountain, they saw a fire in the southwest direction and they knew that their cabin was burning, and their two children probably burned to ashes. Hastening their speed they happily met the children coming to meet them, unharmed. This was a long, sad winter for them. All their families moved to Gott's Island and made all things common; fish, clams and some game helped them through the winter.

Mr. Gott, with his two sons, Charles and David, was drowned by the capsizing of a boat while returning from the fishing grounds, July 7, 1814. Mr. Gott, sr., was near fifty-five years of age. After his death his widow married Peter Gott, of Swan's Island, in the year 1824. Peter then lived at Gott's Island until his second wife's death, when he returned to Swan's Island, and lived with his sons there until his death in 1839.

Daniel and Hannah Gott were the parents of twelve children, all of whom reached adult age, married and had large families of their own. There were ninety-seven grandchildren, of whom eighty-one were married. Of these eight were married the second time. The following were the children — eight sons and four daughters. The daughters were: Hannah, wife of William Appleton, who settled at Tremont; Elizabeth, wife of James Somes, who settled at Beech Hill; Mary, born in 1775, married her cousin, Amos Thurston, and settled at Deer Isle; Sarah, born May 26, 1786, married Solomon Thurston, and settled at Fox Island; she died August 23, 1869. The sons were: Daniel, jr., Nathaniel, Joseph, Benjamin, William, Charles, David and Isaac.

The families of the children of Daniel and Hannah Gott will be further noticed.

I. Daniel Gott, jr., in 1785 married Deborah Richardson, and settled at Beech Hill. They were the parents of nine children as follows: Daniel, who died at the age of twenty-one; Susannah, who married, Dec. 21, 1809, Rufus Wasgatt; Sarah, who married, Nov. 30, 1815, Asa Wasgatt; Nathaniel, who married, in 1814, Jane Dodge; Deborah, who became the second wife of Daniel Ladd; Eliza, who was the first wife of Daniel Ladd; Benjamin, who died unmarried; all the above settled at Beech Hill; Isaac, who married Mrs. Tryphosa Atherton; after her death he married Margaret Richardson and settled at West Ellsworth; Ann, who married Luther Park, and moved out West.

II. Nathaniel Gott was born Feb. 11, 1765. His wife was Betsey Richardson, who was born April 14, 1767. They were married November 28, 1786. He settled on Gott's Island. They were the parents of twelve children, all of whom but one married and reared large families. Mr. Gott died January 27, 1841. His wife died March 15, 1844.

The following were their children — one son and eleven daughters: Asenath, wife of Philip Moore, of Gott's Island; Jane, wife of James Greening, of Southwest Harbor; Lucinda, wife of Thomas Stanley, of Little Cranberry Isle; Esther, wife of Philip Longley, of Southwest Harbor; Clarissa, wife of William Gilley, of Cranberry Isles; after his death she became the wife of David

Cates, of the same town; Hannah died unmarried; Deborah was the wife of John Clark, of Beech Hill; Nathaniel, jr., married Huldah Hudlock and settled at Gott's Island; Rhoda, wife of Daniel Hamblen, of Bass Harbor; Betsy, wife of Nicholas Tinker, of Southwest Harbor; Mary, wife of Benjamin Richardson, of Somerville; Judith, who was the first wife of Mr. Cates.

III. Hannah Gott was the wife of William Appleton. They settled at Tremont. They were the parents of the following six children: Hannah, wife of a Mr. Davis, of Ohio; Polly, wife of Robert Nichols; Reuben married Jane ——— ; after his death she became the wife of Alfred Harper; Charles died unmarried; Sally, wife of William Reed, of Goose Cove, Tremont; Betsy, wife of William Harper, of Tremont.

IV. Elizabeth Gott married James Somes and settled at Beech Hill, where all their children were born. They afterwards moved to Solon, Maine, where they died — Mr. Somes at the age of sixty-eight years and his wife at the age of sixty years. They were the parents of nine children — three sons and six daughters, as follows: Hannah, wife of Stephen Manchester; they settled at Solon; Naomi died in Bangor unmarried; Sarah, wife of Benjamin Merrill, of Solon; Elizabeth married Daniel Durrill, who settled in Los Angeles, Cal.; his widow still resides there; Mary died in infancy; Mary, another child of that name, was the wife of Ezra Averill; they settled at Twin Lake, Mich.; James married Louisa Wright and settled in Dry Creek, Cal.; they are both living; Abram died in Florence, Cal.; Daniel G. married Charlotta L. Thorn and settled in Los Angeles. There are only three of this family now living (1895) — Elizabeth, aged eighty-two, James, aged seventy-seven, and Daniel, aged sixty-nine years.

V. Mary Gott married her cousin, Amos Thurston, of Deer Isle. (Mary's mother, Eunice, was a sister of Daniel Gott, of Gott's Island. She married John Thurston, of Gloucester, who settled at Deer Isle in 1784.) Mr. and Mrs. Amos Thurston were the parents of eight children. They owned a large part of the land on which the village of Oceanville is now located. Mrs. Thurston died in 1866, at the advanced age of ninety-one years. For many years before her death she was totally blind. Their children were: Mary, born in 1798, died in 1803; Eunice, born in 1800, married Edward Small, of Deer Isle; Susan, born in 1802, married John Webster Small, of Deer Isle, December 7, 1820; Mr. Small died in 1874, aged seventy-four years; Mrs. Small died in 1889, aged eighty-seven years; Mary, born in 1804, married Nathaniel H. Richardson, of Somesville, in 1826; Ambrose, born in 1806, married Serena Morrill Gott; Amos, born in 1809, married Ann Stinson, of Deer Isle; Elizabeth, born in 1815, married Walter Butler Hamblen; after his death she became the wife of Capt. Jesse Stinson; Hannah Ann, born in 1819, died in 1836.

VI. Joseph Gott married Lydia Barton and settled at Little Gott's (Bar) Island. They were the parents of nine children, viz.: Joseph, jr., married Hannah Carter (a sister of David Gott's wife); Lydia was the wife of William Hopkins; Ruth was the wife of Francis Gilley, of Orland; Daniel married Lydia Benson; after her death he married Cornelia Dodge; Joanna was the wife of Daniel Robinson, of Southwest Harbor; James married Hulda Dawes; Martha was the wife of Earl Lane; Hannah was the second wife of Earl Lane; Robert married Rebecca Robinson, after her death he married a Mrs. Ober.

VII. Benjamin Gott married, in 1796, Lydia Morgan, and settled at Bass Harbor. They were the parents of nine children as follows: Lydia, born in 1797, married Robert Mitchell, of Placentia; Benjamin died unmarried; Joseph married Martha Gott and settled at Goose Cove; Susan married Josiah Leach; David married Susan Kelley, and lived at Goose Cove; John, born in 1812, married Nancy T. Gott, who was born in 1819; Ezra was lost at sea; Ellen married and lived in Boston; Elizabeth married John Dawes; after his death she became the wife of a Mr. Hodgdon.

VIII. William Gott was born Oct. 17, 1777. He married Susannah Milliken Nov. 3, 1806, and settled at Gott's Island. They were the parents of five children. Mr. Gott died Feb. 17, 1856; his wife died June 6, 1856. Their children were: William, who married Mary Smith; Samuel, who married Hannah Richardson and settled at Gott's Island; Daniel, who died unmarried; Salome, who was the wife of Abram Morrison; Phœbe, who was the wife of Daniel Jordan, of Orland; Susan, who was the wife of Daniel Rich, of Bass Harbor.

IX. Charles Gott was born in 1771; married Susan Thurston; after her death, which occurred in 1808, at the age of twenty-seven years, he married Mrs. Lois Hooper, a sister of his first wife. Mr. Gott was drowned, together with his father and brother David, July 7, 1814, at the age of forty-three years. His widow moved to Sedgwick where she reared her family. There were eight children, as follows: Susanna, born 1798, died 1817; Lois T., born in 1800, was the wife of David Walker; she died in 1886; Nancy F., born in 1802, was the wife of John Thurston, of South Deer Isle; Amos T., born in 1805, married Joanna Gott, a daughter of David Gott; after her death he married Mrs. Margaret M. (Douglass) Gott, widow of Solomon Gott; Charles jr., born in 1807, married Alice Carter, of Sedgwick. The children by his second wife were: Solomon T., born in 1810, married Margaret Douglass; Eunice T., born in 1812, married Joseph Herrick, of Sedgwick; Hannah, born in 1813, was the wife of Daniel Douglass.

X. David Gott married Joanna Carter and settled on Gott's Island. He was drowned, as stated in the last notice, July 7, 1814. His widow moved to Bluehill, where she reared her family of four children. They were: Abigail, wife of Moses Friend, of Sedgwick; Joanna, wife of Amos Thurston Gott; Hannah married in 1832 Preston Preble; Mrs. Preble is still living in Sedgwick at the age of eighty-three years (1895); David, jr., died in infancy.

XI. Sarah Gott born in 1786, married Solomon Thurston. They were the parents of nine children. Mr.

Thurston died in 1854, aged seventy-one years; his wife died August 23, 1869. Their children were: Sarah, born in 1809, was the wife of Enos Cooper, of Rockport; Solomon, born in 1811, married Mary Annis; after her death he married Calista Calderwood; Martha was the wife of Jesse Thayer, of West Deer Isle; Hannah was the wife of James Witherspoon, of North Haven; Sophronia was the wife of William Harrison Smith; John married Lizzie Grindle, of North Haven; Daniel was lost at sea in 1848; Mary Ann married, in 1832, J. W. Ingraham; William married Abbie Wright, of Rockland.

XII. Isaac Gott married his cousin, Mary Thurston, and settled at Bass Harbor. They were the parents of eight children, as follows: Mary, wife of John Verrill; Isaac, who married Betsy Thurston, of Deer Isle; Serena was the wife of Ambrose Thurston, of Deer Isle; James, who married Martha Small, of Deer Isle; after her death he married Eliza Webster, of Goose Cove; Hannah was the wife of Sullivan Webster; Mary was the wife of John Gott; Lydia died unmarried; Almira T. was the wife of Ambrose Thurston, of Tremont.

RICHARDSON FAMILY.

Four Richardsons married Gotts, both parties of whom came from Gloucester, as we have before noticed.

I. James Richardson married Rachel Gott, and settled at Somesville. Their children were: Polly, who married Ezra Gott, and settled at Seal Cove, Tremont; Judith, who married John Somes, of Somesville; Rhoda was the wife of Reuben Freeman, of Pretty Marsh; Tamezin, born in 1772, married George Freeman, of Pretty Marsh; Rachel married David Wasgatt; George, born August, 1763, was twice married; his second wife was Mrs. Betsy (Martin) Simons; James, jr., married a Miss Sargent; after her death he married Hannah Gilpatrick; Daniel married Sarah Cousins; Elijah left home when young, and never returned. The above George Richardson was the first child born to settlers on Mount Desert. The marriage of Rachel and David Wasgatt was the first solemnized on Mount Desert; it was on August 9, 1774; the ceremony was performed by Rev. Daniel Little, of Kennebunk.

II. Stephen Richardson married Elizabeth Gott. Their children were: Stephen, jr., who married Margaret Webster; John, who married Sarah Gamage; after her death he married Hannah (Wasgatt) Day; Deborah married, in 1785, Daniel Gott, jr., of Gott's Island; Hannah married Daniel Hamblen; William married Lucy Hudlock.

III. Thomas Richardson married Margaret Gott. Their children were: Thomas, who married Amy Rich; Abram, who married Mercy Wormell; Puah, wife of Peter Gott, jr.; Enoch (no record); Cornelius, who married Margaret Richardson.

This is a complete record of the Gott family that came from Gloucester for three generations after their settlement.

Daniel Hamblen came to Gott's Island from Deer Isle, where he had previously lived. His wife was Hannah Richardson. They were the parents of nine children: Sarah married Stephen Richardson, and settled at Mount Desert; Elizabeth was the wife of Richard Carpenter, who settled on Swan's Island; after his death she became the wife of Ephraim Emerson, of Bucksport, and after his death she became the wife of Charles Wheeler, of Carmel; Daniel, jr., married Rhoda Gott; they lived at Placentia, and later moved to Deer Isle; Walter died at the age of four years; Hannah was the wife of Alfred Babbidge, who settled on Swan's Island; later they moved to Rockland; Mary C. was the wife of Joseph S. Babbidge, of Swan's Island; Walter Butler married Margaret Gott, of Gott's Island; after her death he married Elizabeth Thurston, of Deer Isle; John and Susan were twins; John was lost at sea at the age of nineteen years; Susan was the wife of Augustus R. Staples, of Swan's Island.

CHAPTER VI.

THE FISHING INDUSTRY.

From time immemorial it has been an honorable calling " to those that went down to the sea in boats ". These brave and hardy mariners, inured from early life to exposure and countless dangers, acquire a courage and calmness in the hour of peril that are sublime. The brilliant and daring achievements of our little navy in its unequal contest with the " Mistress of the Sea " in 1812-14, which attracted the notice and compelled the respect of the whole world, were made possible by our plucky seamen who manned those ships.

In the future, when warfare will be practically settled on the ocean, this country will not turn in vain to our brave sailors and fishermen to defend the nation's honor in the time of peril. For this reason the interests of the mariners have always been watched with the greatest solicitude, and their rights jealously protected both by national laws and international treaties since the foundation of the government.

The fisheries at Swan's Island must have begun with, and, in fact, led to, its settlement; in after years they became the sole means of support to its inhabitants. Few, if any other town in the State, ever had its entire population dependent upon one industry for a livelihood. During the first half century after its settlement, and even later, every man and boy in this town was perfectly familiar with and had been employed on a boat or vessel in this dangerous but oftentimes lucrative employment of following the sea.

Most of the settlers who came here had been fishermen in the places from which they came, and their chief attraction here was the abundance and variety of fish that could be caught near the shore, and the excellent harbor which afforded shelter for their boats. Even those who were engaged for a time in cutting and hauling logs that were manufactured at Swan's mills, soon began to see a more lucrative employment in the shore fisheries, which industry was beginning to be stimulated by a demand in the market.

Even in those early times, with what could be earned from the fisheries, with the crops that could be raised from the fairly productive soil, and cutting kiln-wood in the winter, the settler could make ample provision for his family. Others engaged in freighting Swan's lumber to market. Among those who came here for this purpose were the Nutters, Kents and Sadlers. Kiln-wood was carried to what is now the city of Rockland, where lime-burning had begun. Paving stones taken from the surf-worn beaches of the outer shores were disposed of in the older towns of Massachusetts. Traders came here in vessels from a distance, and offered liquor, manufactured articles and other wares in exchange for such products as could readily be handled, such as dried fish, wool and such products of the soil as could be spared.

Near the year 1800 the market for salt fish increased,

and the price was good considering the ease with which they could be taken; the business drew the attention of the settlers more and more to this means of obtaining a livelihood. Unfortunately their lack of the means to engage in the business on a large scale, as well as a lack of knowledge of the business conditions at a distance, prevented them from securing the profit they otherwise could have made. Years elapsed before anything larger than open boats were used at this island. Both the boat and the mode of fishing were of the most primitive character. The largest boats were called chebacco boats. They were small two-masted boats of about fifteen tons. Cod and haddock were the only fish for which there was a call in the market. Halibut were plenty, often so abundant as to make it necessary for a boat to change her berth to avoid them, but they were not marketable. Occasionally a fisherman would catch one and smoke it for use in his own family. The larger part of the fishing, however, was done in small row-boats called wherries. The fishermen would usually get an early start so as to be on the fishing grounds by daylight. Often a large number of boats would go out in company. Here they would fish with hand lines until near sundown, when they would get up their killick and start for the harbor.

When brought to shore the fish were split, dressed and thoroughly washed, then carried on a hand barrow to the little fish-house where they were salted. During the day women spread the fish on flakes to dry, turning them to dry both sides alike and often shading them with green boughs in the heat of the day to save them from being burned by the sun. When sufficiently cured, they were stored in the loft of the fish-house until fall when they were carried to market and exchanged for shoes, clothes and provisions to last the family through the long, bleak winters. The fisherman's wife found few moments in the day to be idle. Besides the care of a large family of children, she carded, spun and wove the wool into cloth for the use of the family; and, with the aid of the children, planted a little garden, tending it whenever there was a spare moment. In the fall she would gather in a good harvest to reward her for her toil. Such hardships and privations of these pioneer settlers on these inhospitable shores, and the firm and cheerful willingness and power to overcome all these obstacles, have certainly transmitted to their descendants on this island the thrift, frugality and self reliance which have been the means of surrounding them with homes of comfort and luxury.

Many of the early settlers here were boat-builders. They could get out their building material from the forest around them, and work on boats during odd hours in the winter when they could not go out fishing. Moses Staples not only built boats for home use, but also small vessels, which he sold to people from other places. The Joyces were also ship carpenters.

An increase in the demand and supply of fish called for boats of larger capacity, for better fishing grounds were found farther off shore, where it was unsafe to go in small boats; besides, the latter were inconvenient in carrying their fish to market. So about the year 1810 the chebacco boat was succeeded by the jigger or pinky. The pinky had a small cuddy wherein were berths for the crew, a brick fireplace and chimney with a wooden funnel. Their food consisted mainly of fish, potatoes, pork, molasses and Indian or barley bread. In these small crafts some long and hazardous voyages were made. This was especially risky in returning from the gulf of St. Lawrence in the fall of the year, when they would often encounter severe gales where no harbor could be made, and the only alternative was to withstand the tempest as best they could, or go to their destruction on that rockbound shore. It seems almost miraculous that no more accidents occurred at that time.

Mackerel were first caught in 1800. At first little attention was paid to this kind of fish, but year by year mackerel fishing grew in importance. In 1816 the jig hook was invented by Abraham Lurvey. The earliest practice of catching mackerel was for the vessel to drift slowly under light sail, with the crew ranged along the side of the vessel or boat, each with a hook and line attached to a pole held in the hand. The hook being baited and flung out to a length of several yards, and it moving through the water, attracted the attention of the mackerel, which, upon being caught, were landed on board and thrown into a barrel or tub. It was discovered later that throwing chopped menhaden or herring into the water had the effect of attracting the mackerel in great numbers. The oily portion of the bait covering the surface of the water, acted as a guide for the fish to follow until, reaching the side of the vessel, they came in contact with the hooks baited with fresh and more palatable bait which was ravenously seized by the mackerel. Bait mills, to grind up the fish, came into use in 1820. This was a great labor-saving device, as previous to this time the fish had to be chopped with a hatchet. Poles to which lines were attached while fishing were soon dispensed with as being cumbersome and unnecessary. Soon any sized boat, from a skiff to a pinky, was serviceable for catching mackerel. Skill in catching was the main consideration. In getting crews, boys from twelve to twenty were more often selected as being more proficient than those of more mature years. This employment of boys made the burden of raising large families easy, when they were composed mostly of boys. A separate account was kept of each man's catch, so the more skillful he was the greater would be his income. One half of the gross stock went to the owners of the vessel who furnished the supplies and provisions, and the other half went to the crew. Some years, even in these small crafts, excellent year's work was made.

Quite a number of pinkies were owned here, among them were the "Columbia", owned by Levi Torrey, the schooner "Amelia", owned by Benjamin Stinson, the "Pearl", "Young James", "Catherine", built by Silas Hardy, and the "Arcade", built by Ebenezer Joyce and Alexander Staples in 1827.

Vessels engaged in mackerel fishing would fit out in

March or April to go south and return about the first of July. The rest of the season would be spent in the bay of Fundy and along the whole coast of Maine, and some even went to the gulf of St. Lawrence. Codfishing, however, continued to be the principal fishery.

Recognizing the great service of the fishermen in the war, and wishing to further encourage this industry, Congress passed an act on July 29, 1813, to pay a bounty to vessels so employed. The following is a synopsis of that law: That after the last day of December, 1814, there shall be paid to the owners of vessels carrying on the bank and other cod fisheries who have been employed therein at sea for four months in the year, the following bounty: For vessels between 20 and 30 tons, $2.40 per ton; above 30 tons, $4, of which three-eighths shall go to the owners of the vessel, and five-eighths divided among the crew. The amount allowed to any one vessel was not to exceed $272. At the same time a bounty was granted to fishing-boats of more than five and less than twenty tons, provided said boat landed a quantity of fish equal to twelve quintals for every ton of measurement. The codfish industry reached its height about 1832, after which it gradually declined. The bounty laws were repealed July 28, 1866.

As the other fisheries declined, the mackerel catch increased, the common practice being to engage in codfishing, getting one fare before the mackerel appeared, either on the Maine coast or in the gulf of St. Lawrence, after which the vessel, and usually the same crew, would engage in mackerel fishing.

A day's experience on board of a hand-line mackerel fisherman of those times is so graphically described by Aaron Lightfoot that I give it below:

"The amount of moral courage and Christian fortitude required for a landsman to get up out of a comfortable bed and struggle up on a cold, wet, cheerless deck to handle cold, wet lines and colder, wetter fish, all for the 'experience', will never be known except by those who have allowed themselves to be deluded into the thing. It is diabolical. Now the mainsail is up, the jib down, and the captain is throwing bait. It is not yet quite light, but we hear other mainsails going up all around us. A cold drizzling rain does not add to the comfort of the situation, and we stand around shivering, half asleep, with our sore hands in our wet pockets, about as 'demmed moist, uncomfortable bodies', as ever dear old Mantilini saw, and all wishing we were at home, and had never heard of a mackerel. The skipper, however, is holding his line over the rail with an air that clearly intimates that the slightest kind of a nibble will be quite sufficient this morning to seal the doom of the unfortunate mack.

"'There, by Jove! the captain's hauling back—I told you so! Skipper's got him—no—ah, captain, you hauled back too savagely!'

"With the first movement of the captain's arm indicating the presence of fish, everybody rushes madly to the rail, and jigs are heard on all sides splashing into the water, and eager hands and arms are stretched at their full length over the side, feeling anxiously for a nibble.

"'Sh—hist! there's something just passed my fly—I felt him,' says an old man standing alongside of me. 'Yes, and I've got him!' triumphantly shouts the next man on the other side of him, hauling in, as he speaks, a fine mackerel, and striking him off into the barrel in the most approved style.

"Z-z-z-zip goes my line through and deep into my poor fingers, as a huge fellow rushes savagely away with what he finds is not so great a prize as he fondly supposed. I was greatly flurried, missed stroke half a dozen times in as many fathoms of line, and at length succeeded in landing my first fish safely in my barrel, where he lies floundering, 'melancholy and melodious,' as my next neighbor styles it.

"Daylight soon dawns, and the rain, which had been threatening very moistly all night, began to pour down in dead earnest; and as the big drops began to patter in the water the fish began to bite furiously.

"'Shorten up,' says the skipper, and we shorten our lines to about eight feet from the rail to the hooks, when we can hook them in just as fast as we can move our hands and arms. 'Keep your lines clear!' is now the word, as the doomed fish flip faster and faster into our barrels. Every face wears an expression of anxious determination. Everybody moves as though he had a full set of elastic springs within him; every heart beats loud with excitement, and every hand hauls in fish and throws out hook with a method: cool precision, a kind of slow haste, which unites the greatest speed with the utmost security against foul lines.

"The rain momentarily increases. We hear jigs rattling down, and glancing up hastily, I am surprised to find our vessel surrounded on all sides by the fleet, which has already become aware that we have fish alongside.

"Meantime the wind rises, the sea struggles against the rain, which is endeavoring with its steady patter to quiet the turmoil of Old Ocean. We are already on our third barrel of fish, each, and still they come as fast as ever, and the business (sport it ceased to be some time ago) continues with undiminished vigor. Streams of perspiration course down our faces. Jackets, caps and even our shirts are thrown off to give greater freedom to limbs that are worked to their utmost.

"'Hello! where are the fish?' calls out somebody; and sure enough, all at once the whole business comes to a standstill — the fish have apparently 'shut up shop' and gone home, for not the faintest nibble does one of the fishermen get. The mackerel, which a moment ago were fairly rushing on board, have in that moment disappeared so completely that not a sign of one is left. The next vessel under our lee holds them a little longer than we, but they finally also disappear from her side. And so on all around us.

"And now we have a chance to look around us; to compare notes on each other's success; to straighten our backbones, nearly broken and aching horribly with constant reaching over; to examine our fingers, cut to pieces and grown as sensationless as a piece of salt junk, with the perpetual dragging of small lines across them."

About the year 1850 a decided improvement in the moral and social condition of the people of Swan's Island took place. Increased economy resulted in placing some of the settlers in a position to obtain better fishing crafts, and the bounty paid by the government greatly stimulated the industy here. This saved the necessity of running in debt in advance for the necessaries of life and the expense of running the craft. Improved methods of fishing were learned from the crafts of the larger ports of Massachusetts, New Hampshire and Maine, and at the outbreak of the Civil war quite a number of fair-sized vessels were owned by their captains here. The high price for fish caused by the war resulted in increased production, and a steady growth in prosperity was maintained for several years. Several captains here accumulated considerable property, and the lesson learned from them resulted in profitable returns to the generation succeeding them.

The following is a list of vessels belonging to Swan's Island which were registered at the custom-house at Castine at the close of the war: Schooners "Clarissa Ferson", "Eagle", "Eliza Mary", "Emerald", "Empire", "Gipsy Queen", "Golden Rule", "Huntress", "Ivy", "John Pew", "Lucy May", "Matilda", "Orinole", "Phebe", "Rainbow", "Reindeer", "S. J. Collins", "Sharpshooter", "Shawmut", "Traveler", "Traverse" and "Volant". In tonnage they ranged from ten to sixty tons.

About the year 1871 a new mode of catching mackerel was instituted. Instead of the hook and line, large, expensive seines began to be used. The first to try this new experiment from this island was Capt. Freeman Gott in the schooner "Highland Queen" during the season of '72. So many more fish could be taken in this way, that the other vessels quickly supplied themselves with the necessary apparatus. Much more capital became invested in this industry. New, fast-sailing vessels were built, and expensive seines and seine-boats were required.

Stern discipline as seen on a merchant ship does not exist on board a fisherman. Of the sixteen to eighteen men that comprise her crew, all are on equal terms, the captain often consulting with the crew, and all working with a will and in harmony, as the income depends on the activity of every man. The crew is composed mostly of Americans, who are active and experienced fishermen. The food served aboard these seiners is as good as at a hotel. The cabin is finished and furnished in a tasteful and often elegant manner. The share is managed differently from what it was on a hand liner, as the crew of the seiner usually all share the same. One-half of the proceeds is thus divided among the crew, and the other half goes to furnish supplies and gear, and to compensate the owners of the vessel.

Mackerel seiners usually collect in a fleet. Often a hundred or more sail of vessels will be in view of each other at one time on the fishing grounds, or together seek the shelter of some friendly harbor during a storm. Such a fleet entering or leaving a harbor presents a most interesting view.

Mackerel having been fed on bait so long a time had become very tame, so that they would collect in great bodies, called schools, which would appear near the surface of the water. A lookout is kept at masthead. As soon as a school is seen by him, all is excitement on board the vessel. The seine-boat is manned by some ten men, who row rapidly toward where the mackerel are showing. When in the right position the seine, of about 1,500 feet, is cast in a circle around the fish, and the bottom of the seine is then pursed up. The vessel is speedily brought alongside the seine-boat, and a portion of the cork line is fastened to the rail of the vessel, so that the mackerel lie in the seine between the vessel's side and the seine-boat. A large dip-net with tackle and a long handle soon bails the mackerel out, by the half barrelful, on the deck.

Next begins the dressing of the mackerel. With a small dip-net they are thrown into square boxes, where they are split, gibbed and finally salted into barrels. The fish is also often cut by slight curves called "plowed", which gives them a fat appearance. Sometimes the seine is thrown many times a day. Often the mackerel get frightened and escape under the seine before it is pursed up; again two or three hundred barrels may be taken at one time.

Fishermen from Swan's Island soon took a leading place in this industry. Their knowledge of net fishing, previously gained in the herring and other fisheries, made them well qualified to operate the purse seine successfully. Especially during the first two or three years our vessels were noted for their phenomenal catches, from which sufficient profit was made to enable them to buy and own, even then, ten to fifteen of the best vessels in the fleet.

From 1874 to 1889 Swan's Island fishing vessels took either the first or second place every year among the fleet of the whole Atlantic coast, a fact that should awaken an honest pride in the energy and thrift of our fishermen. Many large and expensive vessels were built for and owned by our captains, and seamen came from all the surrounding towns to secure positions with our successful captains. Signs of prosperity were everywhere apparent. New, elegant houses were rapidly being erected. Roads were improved, and many horses were brought to the island. Travel greatly increased so that it made it profitable for a steamboat to connect here. No pauper called for aid; everybody had a plenty. So alluring and profitable was this occupation that almost every male inhabitant, except those enfeebled by old age or the young boys, would be gone from the island.

Among some of the notable fares it may be noticed that in 1880 the schooner "Alice", of Swan's Island, took 3,700 barrels of mackerel, stocking $19,548.75. In 1881 the schooner "Isaac Rich" took 2,000 barrels up to the middle of July. The same year the schooner "Alice" took 4,804 barrels to Oct. 21. In 1885 the steamer "Novelty", built for and commanded by Hanson B. Joyce, was one of the largest fishing steamers in the world, carrying a crew of forty men. Although very large quantities of mackerel were taken, yet the expense of running her was large. Unfortunately about this time the mackerel, which had been so persistently chased, began to disappear. This made the experiment with the steamer rather unprofitable, so in 1889, after a four years' trial, she was sold at a considerable loss. From this time until 1891 this industry gradually declined. After this time the decline in the quantity obtainable and the difficulty of keeping track of so small a body of fish, made success more a matter of luck and circumstances than of energy and hard work. Finally, one by one, the vessels were disposed of until at this time none is owned here, and the fishermen have found new occupations.

Below is given a list of our successful commanders and the vessels they sailed. Most of them sailed the same vessels in different years, but to save repetition I have used the name of the vessel only once, giving the preference to the owner. Vessels owned wholly or in part in this town are in italics:

Capt. George Barbour, schrs *John Nye* and *Queen of the West*.
Capt. B. J. Staples, schr *Golden Rule*.
Capt. E. M. Staples, schrs Cherokee, Andrew W. Dodd and Petrel.
Capt. John S. Staples, schrs Joseph Story, Annie E. Friend, Eliza R., *John Somes*, Vesta, Laura Belle and James Dyer.
Capt. W. Leslie Joyce, schrs Lillian M. Warren and Rambler.
Capt. Charles Staples, schrs *Corporal Trim* and *Miantonomah*.
Capt. Edwin Joyce, schrs Eliza K. Parkhurst, Henry L. Phillips, William H. Oakes, A. T. Giffard, Moro Castle and W. R. Crittenden.
Capt. William S. Joyce, schrs Esperanza and William D. Daisley.
Capt. Emery E. Joyce, schrs *Highland Queen*, *Robert Pettis*, Sir Knight, and F. H. Smith.
Capt. Andrew C. Smith, schrs Warren J. Crosby, Richard Lester, Annie M. Nash, Mayor Jones, *George F. Keene* and *Henry Morganthan*.
Capt. Alvah Barbour, schrs William H. Cross and Emma,

also passenger steamers *Mayfield*, Florence and Vinalhaven.

Capt. Hanson B. Joyce, schrs *G. W. Reed, Lizzie Williams, Alice, Willie F. Joyce, Solitaire* and steamer *Novelty*.

Capt. Michael Stinson, schrs *Lucy J. Warren, Charlotta Augusta, Franklin Pierce, Thomas Hunt, Amelia Cobb* and *Lizzie Poor*.

Capt. William P. Herrick, schrs Pioneer, Amos Cutter, *Rebecca S. Atwood*, Cayenne, *Augusta E. Herrick*, and Ellie T. Kempt.

Capt. Charles E. Sprague, schrs *Vanelia*, G. W. Bentley, Benjamin S. Wright, Charles Kelley, Annie Freeman, Georgie Willard and Hannah Stone.

Capt. Frank Sprague, schrs *C. D. Oliver*, Aeronaut and Isaac Chapman.

Capt. Leroy Smith, schrs Winnie Webster, Old Chad, Lucy W. Dyer, George W. Brown, and *Fairy Frost*.

Capt. John C. Kent, schrs *Sparkling Billow* and Mary Amanda.

Capt. Daniel McKay, schrs Vanelia and Robert D. Rhodes.

Capt. James McKay, schrs Ellen Lincoln, Maud D. Witherell and Ellen F. Dority.

Capt. Edmond F. Bridges, schr *Glad Tidings*.

Capt. Reuben Stewart, schr D. D. Gyer.

Capt. William Stewart, schr Belle Haskell.

Capt. Llewellyn V. Joyce, schrs M. M. Chase and Lady Elgin.

Capt. Freeman Kent, schrs Nellie Woodbury, J. S. Glover and Hattie Western.

Capt. Herbert Holbrook, schr Maggie Powers.

Capt. Augustine Holbrook, schr D. B. Webb.

Capt. Oliver Lane, schrs Alice M. Gould, Webster and Lalla Rookh.
Capt. John A. Gott, schrs Olive G. Tower, *Isaac Rich* and *Daniel Simmons*.
Capt. Emery K. Gott, schrs Maggie Willard, Abbie M. Deering and George Gilmore.
Capt. Horace E. Stanley, schrs M. E. Torrey and Flying Cloud.
Capt. Hosea Kent, schr Parenthia Davis.
Capt. John Conary, schr John M. Plummer.
Capt. Leander Sprague, schrs A. E. Horton and *John Pew*.
Capt. Frank Gott, schr Ethel Merritt.
Capt. Hardy Stinson, schr J. G. Craige.
Capt. Reuben Joyce, schrs J. F. Chase and Alaska.
Capt. Roland Stewart, schr George Washington.
Capt. Fred Kent, schr Merrimac.
Capt. Otis Stewart, schr Bona Venture.
Capt. Willard Staples, schr Star of the East.

Making in all one hundred and twelve different seiners, of which thirty-four were owned here.

After the mackerel industry had become unprofitable, the class of fishermen who had been there employed turned naturally to some other branch of the fisheries. The most profitable inducement was held out in the lobster fisheries. Few of these fish had been caught previous to 1857. They were then very abundant, especially near the shore. They were of no value except as a fisherman would occasionally catch some for use in his own family. Only the small ones were used as food; the larger ones were thrown away as unfit to be eaten. The superior quality of the lobster as a food began to be appreciated. So about the year 1857 a smack ran between Swan's Island and Boston, but she could not carry and dispose of in the market what three or four men at Swan's Island caught. Generally it was the older men, who were unable to go far from home, who were engaged in catching lobsters.

The difficulty of transporting live lobsters long distances in sailing vessels, led to the establishment of canning factories at various points, one of which was built at Old Harbor. This somewhat stimulated the business. A large number of shore fishermen forsook their former mode of fishing, and turned their attention to catching lobsters for the factory. Prices were low and the supply was usually in excess of the demand. By 1870 prices had to be raised to secure enough for the canning factories, and by 1880 the supply had been reduced so much that the canning factories to some extent were abandoned. Increased steamboat facilities made it practicable to ship live lobsters to the Boston market. In 1890 the demand had greatly exceeded the supply, and prices were consequently gradually raised.

At first only small boats were used, as lobsters could be caught in abundance near the shore. As they grew scarcer larger and larger boats were required to go farther from shore. Now the fishermen have a fine fleet of boats, valued from $100 to $600 each. O. B. Whitten, State commissioner of sea and shore fisheries, informs me that in 1876 there were one hundred and eighteen men engaged in the lobster fisheries some part of the year. The catch was 688,628 lobsters, valued at $56,008.14. In 1897 there were one hundred and forty-two men, who caught 740,967 lobsters, valued at $75,208.56. At the former date all sizes of lobsters were caught and sold, but now it is prohibited by law to sell any less than ten and one-half inches in length. In comparing the above figures it will be seen that there is not only an increase in the gross stock, but also in the catch.

The following is a report of the property engaged in lobster fisheries from this town, and is a conservative estimate :

Number of large boats, 139; valued at $20,850.
" small " 133; " 2,660.
" lobster cars, 139; " 1,390.
" traps (estimated), 50 to a man, at $1 each, 6,950.

Making the property so invested over $30,000.

The porgy fisheries for a time engaged quite a number of our fishermen, and offered luring inducements to invest capital. They were chiefly valued for the oil they contained. Suitable vessels were built, expensive nets bought, buildings and wharves were erected to provide for trying out the oils. Although these fish were so abundant, yet they were so persistently followed and caught by hundreds of small steamers, as well as by boats and vessels of every description, that they suddenly disappeared from the coast, and have never returned. Many of our townsmen lost heavily by this failure, as many had invested nearly all their property in the fishing gear and property that was left useless on their hands. Some it took years of thrift, and others never recovered from these losses.

Shell fish have always been depended upon to supply the necessities of the fishermen when all other sources have been cut off. In fact, it is doubtful if any of these islands would have been settled had it not been for this unfailing source of food supply. The Indians utilized this means of subsistence, as is seen by the immense heaps of clam shells, often forming embankments many feet high. They are also found to considerable depth in the ground, thrown there by some convulsion in nature, or by the gradual settling, caused by the weight added on top. It is said that during the greater part of one winter, owing to the severity of the weather, supplies could not be brought here; the principal food during those weeks of isolation were clams and seabirds. This species of fish has the power of rapid propagation, as it is probable that several crops are hatched and reach maturity during the year. Shell fish have been constantly dug, from the time of the earliest settlement to the present time, without any signs of exhausting the supply.

At first clams were used for food and for bait in fishing. Later they were salted in barrels and disposed of in the markets of other seaports for bait. Since lobster canning has proved unprofitable, many of these factories are canning clams, there being a good market for all that can be produced. At present clams are being shipped in the shell to the Boston market. The income received in this town from shell fish during the year 1897 was $1,500.

A sardine factory was built at Old Harbor in 1895 by H. W. Joyce, which furnishes an excellent market for the abundance of herring, which are found more plentiful near this and adjacent islands than at any other place on the Maine coast. The income from this branch varies from $10,000 to $25,000 per year.

The fishing business will undoubtedly remain, as it has ever been in the past, the main industry in this town, as nature has placed this island in a sea rich with this resource. Other industries, such as the granite works, ice-cutting, etc., may be substituted in part, but the products of the sea are more sought for every year, and while the compensation is adequate, our hardy fishermen can be relied upon to supply the market.

LOST AT SEA.

Lost!
Weary and tempest-tossed,
    Lost at sea!
The ship went down in the foam,
And found a watery home,
While the waves resistless roam
    Wild and free.

Lost!
Trials of fate were crossed,
    Lost at sea!
With seaweed and coral dressed,
And hands crossed o'er his breast,
In a wakeless, dreamless rest,
    Sleepeth he.

Lost!
In ocean's foam and frost,
  Lost at sea!
And no tears fall o'er their grave,
But the restless ocean wave
Roams o'er monarch and o'er slave
  In its glee.

Lost!
The ones we have loved most,
  Lost at sea!
For they may not walk the shore,
When some long, long voyage is o'er,
And they, with us no more,
  Bend the knee.

Lost!
And pallid hands are crossed,
  Lost at sea!
And maidens' eyes are dim,
And mothers' eyes o'erbrim
As they sadly think of him
  In the sea.

Lost!
They are a mighty host,
  Lost in the sea!
And the waves say with their moan,
I am monarch — all I own —
'Tis to me they all have gone —
  Gone to me.

—*S. G. Duley.*

On July 7, 1814, Capt. David Gott and two sons, Charles and David, who went out from Gott's Island to the fishing grounds, were lost by the sudden capsizing of their boat. They had been fishing nearly all day with good success, and were returning when the boat was overturned by a squall, and as the boat was heavily loaded, it sank immediately. When this summer squall had rapidly passed away, no signs of men or boat were to be seen. The father, as well as the two sons, left large families, of whom but one survives at this time — Mrs. Hannah (Gott) Preble, a daughter of David Gott, who now resides in Sedgwick in her eighty-seventh year.

In 1829 Nathan Remick was lost from the schooner "Cornelia", of which his brother, Capt. Reuben Remick, was master. They were returning from Boston where they had been with a load of lumber from Ellsworth. When about fifteen miles out from Cape Ann he had occasion to get into the boat that hung at the davits, when one end of the tackle unhooked, precipitating him into the water. The boat was at once lowered, but in the excitement her painter slipped from their hands, and the boat went beyond their reach, leaving those on board utterly helpless to render assistance. Mr. Remick supported himself in the water and conversed with the crew for some time. Although hatches, boards and everything movable were cast into the sea, none of them reached him. He soon became exhausted and the waves closed over him. He was about twenty years of age, and was to have been married on his arrival home.

In 1831 Samuel Kent was lost while coming from Deer Isle in a sail boat. He had been there for Richard Warren, esq., to perform the marriage ceremony for his son Samuel and Mary Smith. He accidentally fell into the water, and as the wind was blowing and the sea was rough, it was impossible to rescue him.

Capt. John Gott, sr., was lost in 1840. A fishing vessel, under the command of John Gordon, came into Old Harbor on its way to Green's Bank; being rather inexperienced, Capt. Gordon sought the chaperonage of Capt. Gott on this voyage. After much persuasion, Capt. Gott, although near seventy years of age, agreed to accompany him on this voyage, which proved to be their last. When a few days out a terrible gale arose, and the vessel was supposed to have foundered in it, as she was never heard from.

The schooner "Henry M. Johnson", built at this place by her commander, Silas Hardy, was on her first voyage, and had proceeded as far as Eggemoggin Reach where, on account of the storm, they anchored for the night. During the next day, Nov. 7, 1846, the vessel dragged her anchor and went ashore. Capt. Hardy, with his crew, consisting of Abel Staples, 2d, William Torrey and John Ross, took an anchor across the boat to carry it to windward so as to heave the vessel off. They had proceeded but a short way when the boat was capsized in the boisterous sea, and two of the crew, Staples and Ross, lost their lives. Both were young men and married. Mr. Ross's widow afterwards became the wife of William Annis, who was drowned while crossing Stinson Neck bar in February, 1872, at the age of seventy years.

Joshua S. Trask was lost in the Bay of Chaleur during the great gale of October 3, 1851. He was in the schooner "Henry Clay", commanded by Capt. John Walls. The vessel foundered in the gale, and all hands were lost. Mr. Trask was forty-four years of age; he left a widow and six children at this place.

During the same gale Capt. Benjamin Stinson lost his vessel, the "Fly", and Capt. David Smith, 3d, also lost the vessel he commanded — the "Liberator". They were caught in the Bend of Prince Edward's Island; the gale came up so suddenly and with such terrific violence that they were unable to get out of their dangerous location. They were driven with great force upon the sandy beach, but in such a location that no one was lost from either vessel, although the vessels were a total loss. They were both owned at this place.

George Smith was drowned while trying to rescue his brother near Buckle Island in August, 1855.

Gilbert J. Gott was lost at sea February 10, 1860, aged thirty-three years. He was in the schooner "Lawrence N. Dean", and was on the homebound trip of coasting when the vessel was sunk during a snow squall, and was never seen again.

The schooner "Constitution", a vessel owned at this place, was commanded by Seth W. Staples. They had brought home three cargoes of mackerel from the Bay of Chaleur during the season. In the fall they took a load of salted mackerel and smoked herring from Whitmore's and started for Baltimore. Besides the captain there were on board John H. Staples, Daniel H. Babbidge and Allen Reed, all belonging here. On the evening of November 19, 1860, while running down the Cape Cod shore, when about southeast of Nausett light, a squall struck the vessel and capsized her. The captain attempted to save his life by lashing himself to the rigging. The vessel began to settle rapidly. Babbidge and Reed each seized a plank and sprang overboard. Reed alone was saved. Babbidge was undoubtedly drawn down by the suction when the vessel sank. Reed kept himself afloat for over two hours, when he saw the lights of an approaching vessel. They caught the sound of his cries, and although it was very dark, they succeeded in locating him, and took him on board in a nearly exhausted condition. This vessel was the "Isaac Achorn", Capt. Avery.

Ezra Torrey was lost from a small boat June 9, 1865, near the Otto Ponds. He had taken a load of lobster traps and lashed them upon his dory when the boat suddenly rolled over; he was undoubtedly entangled in the gear so as to be unable to reach his boat; his body was not recovered; he left a widow and three children.

On Oct. 12, 1865, Benjamin S. Joyce was knocked overboard and drowned near Port Hood, C. B. He was with his father, Capt. Roderick Joyce, in the schooner "Highland Lass". He was seventeen years of age.

In January, 1867, this town sustained one of the greatest losses of life that ever happened at any one time, in the loss of the schooner "S. J. Collins", owned here and commanded by Winthrop B. Lane. After the fishing season was over, several men with their wives and children made this coasting voyage a trip of pleasure. They took a load of freight at Bangor for New York, after which they took a load of corn at Hoboken, N. J., for Belfast and Bucksport parties. They started for home on Jan. 5. That night a storm and gale came on, and it is supposed the vessel foundered. The vessel's company were Capt. Winthrop B. Lane and wife Emily, who was formerly the wife of Daniel H. Babbidge, who was lost at sea in the schooner "Constitution". Mrs. Lane had with her her two daughters, Lillian Babbidge, aged eight, and Grace Lane, one year old. The others were Simeon S. Reed, his wife Emily and daughter Alice, Joseph F. Reed, aged twenty-five, his wife Isadora, aged twenty-two, and Amos Staples. The whole party were young people.

On November 6, 1869, Edward Warren Gott was lost from a boat near Buckle Isle. He was twenty-three years of age.

Eben Smith was lost from the schooner "Clara Smith", of which he was mate, near the year 1870. They were on the voyage from New York to Havana. They had a deck-load of shooks, which was struck by a sea during a gale. Mr. Smith had just come on deck when the sea swept the deck-load from the vessel, taking him with it.

Capt. John Freeman Gott was lost Nov. 29, 1875, aged thirty-seven years. He was commander of the schooner "John Somes" in which he had been fishing during the summer. He was bound from Portland "down east" for a load of herring. In trying to get into Boothbay harbor they were struck by a squall which capsized the vessel and threw Capt. Gott overboard. He was an enterprising man, and was the commander of the first mackerel seiner from the island.

In December, 1876, the schooner "Modena B. Jerauld", of Gloucester, Capt. Charles P. Mitchell, together with his crew of ten men, was lost on La Have bank. Among the crew was Byron D. Joyce of this place.

Adoniram J. Kent was drowned October 6, 1880, aged thirty years.

Eugene S. Trask was drowned from a small boat June 15, 1881, aged twenty-two years. His body was subsequently recovered.

Reuben C. Bridges was lost in a dory on Middle Bank December 18, 1883. He was in the schooner "J. W. Campbell", Capt. Colin Chisholm. He was twenty-four years of age, and was married just one month before he was lost.

Frank Sprague was drowned by falling overboard at the wharf at Hoboken, N. J., where they had just arrived from South America. He was mate of the schooner, and was superintending the spreading of an awning when the rope on which he was drawing broke and he fell into the water. Before assistance could reach him he was dead. This occurred July 10, 1891. He was thirty-eight years of age.

Hiram Colomy was lost October 10, 1895. He started to row out to Seal Cove to go around Irish point in a small boat. The gale had increased in violence, and the rain had made the boat slippery; it is supposed he fell overboard in his effort to change his position. His brother, coming from Deer Isle, picked up his empty boat and towed her into Old Harbor.

Augustine Holbrook was drowned outside Old Harbor in 1897.

CHAPTER VII.

SYNOPSIS OF THE MUNICIPAL RECORDS.

In 1834 the population of Swan's Island had increased to nearly two hundred inhabitants, and the settlers, having long felt the disadvantages of an unorganized place, thought that the time had come when the number of inhabitants warranted an organization into some local government. Many local matters of considerable moment to the settlers were neglected by the State authorities; roads needed to be built and kept in repair, and, above all, some regular method was needed of furnishing instruction to the young. Concerning the first organization there is no record known to exist. It is supposed that the first record and those of the three following years were burned in a house where the records were kept that was destroyed by fire.

Whether a regular plantation form of government was incorporated according to the requirements of law, or whether the settlers merely met by mutual agreement and chose their officers without any formality, will probably never be known, as no record of their proceedings was made to the secretary of State. Whether this omission was the result of carelessness or not I do not know.

Concerning the year of this organization I am informed by Benj. Smith, esq., who was present at that first meeting, and although but a boy he remembered distinctly not only the year (1834) but also the officers who were then elected. I also find in the record of the meeting held in 1839 that it was voted to abate a tax on Benjamin F. Staples' bills for the year 1834; thus showing that an organization must have existed at that time.

Swan's Island alone constituted this alleged plantation which started on its career in the spring of 1834 at a meeting held in the house of Ebenezer Joyce, where the following officers were elected: Assessors, Benjamin Stinson, Benjamin Smith and James Joyce; clerk, John Stockbridge; treasurer, Benjamin Stinson; collector of taxes, Benjamin F. Staples.. No further record is found until that of the year

1838.

The assessors chosen this year were Augustus R. Staples, Edward Gott and Benjamin F. Stinson.

1839.

Met at schoolhouse in east district. Meeting was opened by prayer by Benjamin Stinson. The following officers were chosen: Benjamin Stinson, moderator and treasurer; Benjamin F. Stinson, clerk; Benjamin Stinson, Augustus R. Staples and James Joyce, assessors: collection of taxes bid off at auction at 3 per cent. by Thomas Sadler. Raised $90 for schools, $150 for roads, and $25 for plantation expenses. William Stanley and Levi Torrey were elected school agents; Benjamin F. Stinson, William Fife and Joseph R. Torrey, school committee; Asa Staples, John Stockbridge and Edward Gott, tythingmen; William Joyce and Enoch Billings sextons.

Voted to abate O'Maley's tax on Benjamin F. Staples' bill for 1834. Voted that no license be given to sell ardent spirits. Voted that the island be divided so that three-fifths of the voters shall be in the west district, and two-fifths in the east district. A road was laid out from John Stockbridge's to Thomas Sadler's house. The tax list this year contained fifty persons.

State election was held September 9, and the following was the vote: For governor, John Fairfield had 19 votes; Edward Kent, 1: for senator, Charles Jarvis, 19; representative to legislature, Allen Hopkins, 19; Amos Clements, 1.

A meeting was called in the west district October 8. They voted to finish their schoolhouse, and raised $60 for the same. The work was set up at auction, and bid off by Edward Gott. School was to begin December 20, and continue eight weeks. Master's board bid off by Thomas Colomy for fifty cents per week. Wood furnished by Benjamin F. Stinson at one shilling per cord. East district voted to have two and one-half months' school in winter, and three months in the summer.

1840.

Augustus R. Staples was chosen moderator; James Joyce, clerk; Benjamin Stinson, Augustus R. Staples and John Stinson, assessors; Benjamin Stinson, treasurer. Voted to pay their taxes in directly to the treasurer. Raised $100 for schools, $150 for highways, and $20 for plantation expenses. Joshua S. Trask and Thomas Colomy were elected school agents: Benjamin F. Stinson, Joseph R. Torrey and Joshua S. Trask, school committee. Voted to lay out a road from the highway to Asa C. Staples' house.

School meeting was held in east district October 14. Voted to begin school the first Monday in January. Master's board bid off by Ebenezer Joyce at $1 a week. In the presidential election held this year the democratic electors had 41 votes, the whigs 3. State election, John Fairfield had 47 votes for governor; Edward Kent 2; representative to the legislature, Thomas Bunker 47; Amos Clements 2.

1841.

Augustus R. Staples, James Joyce and Joseph R. Torrey were chosen assessors. Raised $100 for schools, $30 for current expenses, and $130 for highways. William Joyce and Benjamin Smith were chosen school agents; Augustus R. Staples, Benjamin F. Stinson and Moses Staples, 3d, school committee. Voted to abate the tax on grist-mill. State election, the vote cast was as follows: For governor, John Fairfield 49; Edward Kent 3; representative to the legislature, Amos Allen, 48. At a school meeting it was voted to have two months' school. Board bid off by Moses Staples, 3d, at seventy-two cents a week.

1842.

Benjamin Stinson, William Stinson and Kimball Herrick were chosen assessors. Raised $100 for schools, $30 for current expenses, and $150 for highways. Ebenezer Joyce and Joseph Gott were chosen school agents. Benjamin F. Stinson, John Adams and Silas Hardy, school committee. Voted to divide west district. The southeast district to be formed, the line running between Joseph Gott's and John Gott's; Irish point district line to run between Abel Lane's and David Smith's. William Joyce, William Fife and Joseph Gott were chosen tythingmen. Voted to give east district power to elect its own school agent. State election, John Fairfield had 34 votes for governor; Edward Roberson 1; for representative to the legislature, Stephen Allen 34.

1843.

John Adams, Ebenezer Joyce and Kimball Herrick were chosen assessors; John Adams, Benjamin Stinson and Silas Hardy, school committee. Voted to allow school districts to choose their own agents. Voted to number the districts: West district shall be No. 1, east district No. 2, southwest district No. 3, southeast district No. 4. Raised $100 for schools, $150 for highways, and $40 for current expenses. Voted to lay out a road from Edmond Stanley's to Widow Gott's house. The school committee was allowed fifty cents per school for their compensation. A road to be laid out from the schoolhouse to Silas Hardy's. In district No. 2 voted to pay summer teacher $1.00 per week. At the State election the following vote was cast: For governor, Hugh J. Anderson, 23 votes; representative to the legislature, Erastus Redman, 23.

1844.

Benjamin Stinson, Benjamin Smith, jr., and Joseph R. Torrey were chosen assessors; William Joyce and Samuel Gott tything-men. Raised $125 for schools, $150 for highways and $35 for current expenses. Voted that the assessors lay out a road from William Joyce's to Abel E. Staples' house. At State election the vote was as follows: For governor, Hugh J. Anderson, 45; Edward Robinson, 1; for representative to the legislature, Benjamin F. Stinson, 45; Humphrey Wells, 1. Voted on an amendment to the constitution so as to establish town courts. The votes cast were even—18 yeas and 18 noes. Presidential election, the democratic electors received 60 votes, the whigs 1.

1845.

Augustus R. Staples, Kimball Herrick and William Joyce were chosen assessors. John Adams, Benjamin Smith and Ebenezer Joyce, school committee. Raised $150 for schools, $40 for current expenses, $61 for arrearages, and $150 for highways. Voted not to grant license to sell intoxicating liquors. At the State election the following vote was cast: For governor, Hugh J. Anderson, 40; Freeman H. Morse, 1; representative to the legislature, Hezekiah D. Means, 40. A meeting was called Feb. 14, 1846, at which it was voted to prohibit all non-residents from running hounds, setting traps or laying poison for any fur-bearing animal. The penalty to be $50 fine, one-half of which fine to go to the complainant.

1846.

Augustus R. Staples, Benjamin F. Staples and Kimball Herrick, assessors. Raised $150 for schools, $50 for current expenses, and $150 for highways. Benjamin F. Stinson, Joshua S. Trask and William Fife, school committee. State election the following vote was cast: For governor, John W. Dana, 42; David Bronson, 1; representative to the legislature, Erastus Redman, 42. A meeting was called Feb. 3, 1847, at which it was voted that the men who had been chopping wood on advertised land be allowed to take the wood and pay stumpage according to value—fifty cents for hard wood, and twenty-five for soft wood. These men shall obtain a permit to remove this wood, or they will be liable for trespass. Voted that those claiming the land they occupy shall have the land surveyed, and a record made in the clerk's book. That all other lands not occupied be run out and marked into fifty-acre lots. This survey to be completed before April 30 next. All persons having taken up wild lands shall have the same surveyed and recorded before April 1 next.

1847.

Benjamin Stinson, Augustus R. Staples and Kimball Herrick were chosen assessors. Raised $160 for schools, $50 for current expenses and $150 for highways. No person is to be allowed to hunt with hounds except on his own land. Any person who does not pay tax on the land he has run out shall forfeit his right to said land. Voted to compel every man to keep his sheep within his own enclosure. Accepted the road laid out from Levi Torrey, jr.'s house to the main road.

In this year the wild land which had been advertised was run out by John Dodge, and the following lots were at once taken up: Edmond Stanley, 50 acres; James Sprague 75; John and David Sprague 200; Moses Staples 25; Washington Staples 33; Solomon Barbour 49; Benjamin F. Staples 26; Levi Torrey, jr., 12; Elias Morey 31; Isaiah B. Joyce 10; Benjamin Stockbridge 7; John Stockbridge 31; Ebenezer and Isaiah B. Joyce 151; Joseph Gott 138; Edward Gott 40; Kingsland and Conary 100; Asa C. Staples 25; Benjamin Smith 50; David Smith 115, and Kimball Herrick 115. There were also twenty-two other lots of 50 acres each which were not taken up at this time.

At the State election the votes cast were: For governor, John W. Dana, 35; David Bronson, 1; representative to the legislature, Hezekiah Means, 35; N. K. Sawyer, 1. On the vote to see if the State officers shall be elected by plurality, the result was 26 noes.

1848.

Augustus R. Staples, Benjamin F. Stinson and Benjamin Stockbridge, assessors. Raised $150 for schools, $150 for highways, and $60 for current expenses. Voted to sell non-resident land at auction for cash. Augustus R. Staples was made agent to run off this land and sell it. The lots were marked, according to quality, into first, second and third class. At the State election John W. Dana had 32 votes for governor; Erastus Redman, 36 votes for representative to the legislature. Presidential election the democratic electors had 43 votes; the whig electors 3.

1849.

Kimball Herrick, Benjamin Smith, and Thomas J. Colomy, assessors. Raised $160 for schools, $170 for highways, and $50 for current expenses. Benjamin F. Stinson. Joseph R. Torrey and James Joyce were elected school committee. Ambrose Gott, Edward Gott and Elias Morey, tything-men. Voted to accept the road laid out from Samuel Roberson's to the highway. Voted to divide the money received from wild lands sold, in proportion, according to the inventory of 1846. At the State election John Hubbard received 28 votes for governor; Wyer Sargent 28 votes for representative to the legislature.

1850.

Benjamin Smith, jr., Edward Gott and David Stinson were chosen assessors. School agents chosen were Johnson Billings No. 1, Jacob Reed No. 2, David Stinson No. 3, and David Sprague No. 4. Benjamin F. Stinson, Benjamin Stinson and Edward Gott were chosen school committee. Raised $160 for schools, $175 for roads and $75 for current expenses. The school census in 1850 gave the following result: District No. 1, 64 scholars; No. 2, 62; No. 3, 25; No. 4, 43; total, 194. State election, John Hubbard had 24 votes for governor, William G. Crosby, 3. For representative to the legislature, Stephen D. Gray had 24; Rufus B. Walker, 1, and Rufus K. Walker, 2.

1851.

Kimball Herrick, John Sprague and John Stinson were chosen assessors; Benjamin F. Stinson, Joseph R. Torrey and Augustus R. Torrey, school committee; Benjamin Stinson, the plantation agent to sell wild lands. Raised $150 for schools, $150 for highways and $40 for current expenses. Voted to annex John Gott's property to district No. 1. This year the school census was: District No. 1, 59 scholars; No. 2, 66, No. 3, 21; No. 4, 37. There were at this time 68 voters in the plantation. A special meeting was called for districts Nos. 1, 3 and 4, which voted to lay out a burying ground, funds for the same to be raised by subscription.

1852.

Solomon Barbour, Augustus R. Staples and Thomas Sadler were chosen assessors; Benjamin F. Stinson on the school board. Raised $180 for schools, $175 for highways and $50 for current expenses. At the State election the vote cast was: For governor, John Hubbard, 51; representative to the legislature, William Webb, 56. At the presidential election the democratic electors had 51 votes; whigs none.

1853.

Solomon Barbour, Benjamin Smith, jr., and Joseph R. Torrey were chosen assessors; Augustus R. Torrey was chosen on the school board. Raised $180 for schools, $200 for highways and $60 for current expenses. Voted to lay out a road from Benjamin F. Stinson's house to the highway. State election, vote for governor was: Albert Pillsbury, 12, Anson P. Morrill, 9; William G. Crosby, 2; representative to the legislature, William F. Collins, 15. Voted to accept the road laid out from schoolhouse in district No. 4 to Moses Bridges.

1854.

Benjamin Smith, jr., Benjamin Stinson and Joseph R. Torrey were chosen assessors; Benjamin F. Stinson supervisor of schools. Raised $215 for schools, $200 for highways and $60 for current expenses. The article to provide for the selling of liquor for medicinal purposes was passed over. The number of voters in the plantation this year was 85.

1855.

Kimball Herrick, Asa Joyce and David Stinson were chosen assessors; Benjamin F. Stinson, supervisor of schools. Raised $215 for schools, $125 for highways. Voted that each man shall work out his tax on or before September 20, or shall cause the same to be worked out on the highway. Raised $60 for current expenses. Voted to accept the road laid out from Moses Conary's house to J. S. Smith's barn; also the road from Samuel Kent's to Asa Smith's.

1856.

Augustus R. Staples, Benjamin Smith, jr., and Solomon Barbour were chosen assessors. Voted to have a school committee in place of a supervisor; Benjamin F. Stinson, Augustus R. Torrey and Ebenezer Joyce were chosen. Raised $254 for schools, $200 for highways and $75 for current expenses. State election, the votes cast were: For governor, Samuel Wells, 29; Hannibal Hamlin, 28; representative to the legislature, James Turner, 2d, 29; Charles A. Spofford, 28.

1857.

Solomon Barbour, Benjamin Smith, jr., and John Stockbridge were chosen assessors; Benjamin F. Stinson, Joseph R. Torrey and Ebenezer Joyce, school committee. Raised $260 for schools, $175 for roads, and $75 for current expenses. Voted that districts No. 1 and No. 2 be divided by a line between the property of Edward Gott and Isaiah B. Joyce; that Roderick M. Joyce be annexed to district No. 2, and John Gott to be set off to district No. 1. Number of voters this year was 86. At the State election the vote for governor was: Manassah H. Smith, 19; Lot M. Morrill, 7: representative to the legislature, William Babbidge 19; John Turner 7.

1858.

David Sprague, Benjamin Smith, jr., and John Stockbridge, assessors. Chose Benjamin F. Stinson supervisor of schools. Raised $260 for schools, $75 for current expenses and $150 for roads. The plantation selected the hill near Wharton's as a suitable place to build a schoolhouse, on the north side of the road leading from James Joyce's to B. F. Staples', if a deed can be obtained at a reasonable price. If not it is to be built on land of O. W. Morrey's near said hill.

1859.

Kimball Herrick, Benjamin Smith, jr., and Joseph W. Staples, assessors. The board of assessors be also the school committee. Raised $260 for schools, $75 for current expenses and $150 for highways. Voted to accept road from Lucy Valentine's house to the highway. Voted to divide district No. 1 between David Sprague's and Edward Gott's; the north portion to be known as district No. 5; also that Roderick M. Joyce and others from district No. 2 at the line between J. W. Staples and John S. Joyce, and from district No. 1 to Benjamin Stinson's south line, this new district to be known as No. 6.

1860.

Benjamin Smith, jr., Joseph R. Torrey and Benjamin F. Staples, assessors, the assessors to serve as the school board. Raised $275 for schools, $200 for highways, and $75 for current expenses. At the presidential election the democratic electors had 20 votes and the republican 19.

1861.

Kimball Herrick, Benjamin F. Staples and Benjamin Stockbridge, assessors and school committee. Raised amount of school money required by law; $150 for roads, and $75 for current expenses.

1862.

Benjamin Smith, jr., John Staples and Martin V. Babbidge, assessors. Raised $300 for schools, $80 for current expenses and $150 for highways.

1863.

Same board of assessors as the previous year was elected. Oliver L. Joyce was chosen collector of taxes, and was paid 4 per cent. Martin V. Babbidge, Cornelius Wasgatt and Ebenezer Joyce were school committee. Raised $300 for schools, $75 for current expenses, and $200 for roads. A special meeting was called Dec. 1, at which it was voted to raise $2,100 for volunteers; that the money be hired for two or three years' time, to be obtained in town if possible. Solomon Barbour was chosen agent to raise this money. This year there were 99 voters in the plantation.

1864.

James Joyce, Isaiah B. Joyce and James Joyce, jr., assessors; Cornelius Wasgatt and Martin V. Babbidge, school committee. Voted to instruct the plantation agent to put all bills for war tax into the constable's hands for collection if not paid by September 2. Raised $300 for schools, $50 for current expenses, and $200 for highways. Paid 6 per cent. for collection of taxes. A meeting was called October 24 in which it was voted to raise $5,000 for volunteers and substitutes; that young men liable to be taxed shall pay $50 apiece. Benjamin Smith and Joseph W. Staples were elected collectors. A meeting was called February 17 at which $7,860 was raised to pay the men who have put substitutes in the army under the call of July, 1864. Voted to raise $800 to every man who enlisted.

1865.

Solomon Barbour, Benjamin Smith, jr., and Joseph R. Torrey, assessors; Cornelius Wasgatt, Benjamin Smith, jr., and Joseph R. Torrey, school committee. Raised $350 for schools, $75 for current expenses, and $150 for highways. Voted to accept the road laid out from B. F. Staples' wharf to the nearest highway; also the road from E. F. Smith's to Fred and H. Benson's. A special meeting was called July 10. Heard the report of the men who had put substitutes into the army. Voted to pay them 50 per cent. of what they had paid out, and exempt them from further taxation. Voted to pay the money hired in three yearly installments.

1866.

Solomon Barbour, Benjamin Stockbridge and Oliver L. Joyce, assessors; Cornelius Wasgatt, Joseph R. Torrey and Oliver L. Joyce, school committee. Raised $370 for schools, $75 for current expenses, and voted to pay town officers $1.50 a day; $200 for highways. Voted to tax dogs $5. Voted to accept the road laid out from James Joyce's to Jacob S. Reed's, and thence to the highway at the corner of James Joyce's fence, near Joseph F. Reed's.

1867.

Cornelius Wasgatt, Benjamin Smith, jr., and William Herrick, assessors; Cornelius Wasgatt, Benjamin Smith, jr., and Oliver L. Joyce, school committee. Raised $450 for schools, $75 for current expenses, and $250 for highways. Voted that all road tax not worked out before Oct. 10 to be put in the collector's hands. Chose Jacob S. Reed and Joseph Gott tything-men. Voted that there shall be a town landing at the head of the harbor, near J. Gott's, and a road be laid out to the highway. A meeting was called June 3 at which it was voted to accept the road laid out from Roderick M. Joyce's wharf to the highway near schoolhouse No. 6; also road from John Valentine's dwelling to the highway, and to discontinue the road near Benjamin Stinson's. Aug. 17, there were 96 voters in the plantation.

1868.

Solomon Barbour, Joseph R. Torrey and Isaiah J. Stockbridge, assessors; Cornelius Wasgatt, John V. Stinson and Oliver L. Joyce, school committee. Raised $450 for schools, $40 for current expenses, and $200 for highways. Chose Edward Gott collector of taxes; Levi B. Joyce and James F. Gott tything-men. Number of voters this year was 102. A meeting was called Dec. 5, at which it was voted to pay each man who went from this plantation into the war of the rebellion, or who furnished a substitute, the sum of $100. This amount to be raised in sixty days. At a subsequent meeting this vote was reconsidered, and a longer time given in which to raise $1,500.

1869.

Kimball Herrick, Benjamin Smith, jr., and Joseph R. Torrey, assessors. The first assessor having resigned, John Stockbridge was chosen. Oliver L. Joyce, Martin

V. Babbidge and Joseph R. Torrey, school committee. Raised $500 for schools, $75 for current expenses, and $200 for roads. Levi B. Joyce and Benjamin Smith, jr., were chosen tything-men.

1870.

Cornelius Wasgatt, Kimball Herrick and William Herrick, assessors; Cornelius Wasgatt, James F. Gott and Meltiah J. Stinson, school committee. Raised $500 for schools, $75 for current expenses, and $50 for roads. Voted that the plantation assess and collect $10.50 out of the $1,500, to pay war debt.

1871.

Solomon Barbour, Benjamin Smith, jr., and Meltiah J. Stinson, assessors; Cornelius Wasgatt, Joseph W. Staples and John N. Stinson, school committee. Raised $350 for schools, $100 for highways, $75 for current expenses. Voted to accept road from Kimball Herrick's house to the highway. Voted that district No. 6 be abolished, and that the dividing line between districts No. 1 and 2 be the line between the property of Edward Gott and David H. Sprague.

1872.

Solomon Barbour, Benjamin Smith, jr., and John Stockbridge, assessors; Cornelius Wasgatt, Hanson B. Joyce and Charles H. Joyce, school committee. Raised $450 for schools, $150 for roads. Voted to buy the schoolhouse at Center.

1873.

Hanson B. Joyce, George H. Barbour and Benjamin J. Staples, assessors; Cornelius Wasgatt, Hanson B. Joyce and Charles H. Joyce, school committee, and that the committee be paid $2 per day. Raised $500 for schools, $300 for highways, and $200 for current expenses. Accepted the road laid out from Henry D. Joyce's to Joanna Torrey's house. Voted to change the road that now runs to the northward of E. M. Staples' house so as to run to the southwest of it, commencing at the southwest corner of B. F. Staples' field and meeting the old road in Leslie W. Joyce's pasture. The board of assessors having resigned, Benjamin Smith, Joseph W. Staples and Charles H. Joyce were chosen. In State election Joseph Titcomb had 5 votes; Nelson Dingley, jr., 6.

1874.

Cornelius Wasgatt, Joseph R. Torrey and Benjamin Smith, assessors; Hanson B. Joyce and J. W. Stinson, school committee. Raised $300 for highways, $375 for schools, and $200 for current expenses. Voted that the superintending school committee be authorized to designate what series of text-books shall be used in the schools, and give notice thereof to the parents of the several districts before the summer term of school begins.

1875.

Cornelius Wasgatt, Joseph R. Torrey and Levi B. Joyce, assessors; Cornelius Wasgatt, Martin V. Babbidge and Charles H. Joyce, school committee. James Joyce was chosen collector, his compensation to be $24.50. Raised $500 for schools, $300 for highways and $275 for current expenses.

1876.

David E. Sprague, M. J. Stinson and James Joyce, assessors: Benjamin Smith, collector; Cornelius Wasgatt, Levi B. Joyce and Martin V. Babbidge, school committee. Voted that the treasurer make a discount of 10 per cent. on all taxes paid in previous to November 1, and that all taxes remaining unpaid January 1, 1877, be put in the constable's hands for collection. Raised $400 for schools, $50 for highways and $350 for current expenses. Voted to expend $25 on road leading from Kimball Herrick's house to the highway. The assessors to sell schoolhouse No. 6, and the proceeds divided between districts No. 1 and No. 2 in proportion to the number of scholars which each district received from district No. 6 when this school was discontinued. There were 117 voters in town at this election.

1877.

David E. Sprague, James Joyce and Michael Stinson, assessors; Cornelius Wasgatt, Martin V. Babbidge and Levi B. Joyce, school committee. Raised $400 for schools, $100 for highways, and $375 for current expenses.

1878.

Benjamin Smith, M. J. Stinson and Levi B. Joyce, assessors; John Staples, treasurer; Levi B. Joyce and Charles H. Joyce, school committee. Raised $400 for schools, $375 for current expenses, and $100 for highways. Voted to accept the road laid out from Michael Stinson's house to his wharf, also that the assessors lay out a road from Kimball Herrick's house to the lighthouse on Hocomock Head. A meeting was called March 21, 1878, at which it was voted to discontinue all highways on Swan's Island, and that all money raised for highways be expended on private ways. At the State election the following vote was cast: For governor, Seldon Connor had 3; Joseph L. Smith, 24; Alonzo Garcelon, 12; representative to the legislature, Charles A. Russ had 32; Benjamin G. Barbour, 4. This year there were 139 voters.

1879.

Benjamin Smith, Levi B. Joyce and Oliver L. Joyce, assessors; John Staples, treasurer; Martin V. Babbidge on the school committee. Raised $300 for current expenses, $400 for schools and $200 for roads. At the State election the vote for governor was: Joseph L. Smith, 42; Alonzo Garcelon, 9; Daniel F. Davis, 9; for representative to the legislature, Charles H. S. Webb, 57; Rodney Witherspoon, 9. On the constitutional amendment to have biennial elections for State officers, yeas 57.

1880.

David E. Sprague, James Joyce and Joseph W. Staples, assessors; Joseph W. Staples and Levi B. Joyce, school committee. Raised $400 for current expenses, $400 for schools and $200 for highways. At the State election the vote for governor was: Harris M. Plaisted,

29; Daniel F. Davis, 5; representative to the legislature, Seth Webb, 29; Moses S. Joyce, 5; on constitutional amendment to elect State officers by plurality, yeas 2; noes 10. In the presidential election the democratic electors had 78 votes; the republican 11.

1881.

David E. Sprague, Oliver L. Joyce and Joseph W. Staples, assessors; Levi B. Joyce, Joseph W. Staples and Charles H. Joyce, school committee. Raised $400 for current expenses, $490 for schools, and $400 for highways. Voted that the road laid out by the assessors from Toothaker's by David E. Sprague's to connect with the old road nearly abreast George B. Stewart's, be accepted; also accepted the road laid out past Levi B. Joyce's barn, and running to the old road near the swamp.

1882.

Benjamin Smith, Joseph W. Staples and Myric E. Staples, assessors; Isaiah J. Stockbridge, on the school committee. Raised $490 for schools, $350 for current expenses, and $400 for highways. Voted that all books be bought at the plantation's expense and sold at cost. John Staples was appointed agent. Voted to accept the road laid out from Herbert Joyce's house to the steamboat wharf; also the road from Orlando Trask's house, past John S. Staples' barn to the main road. At the State election the vote stood: For governor, Harris M. Plaisted, 23; Frederick Robie, 7; representative to the legislature, Charles A. Spofford, 23; George H. Howard, 7.

1883.

David E. Sprague, Joseph W. Staples and Isaiah J. Stockbridge, assessors; Levi B. Joyce on the school committee. Raised $500 for highways, $485 for schools, and $400 for current expenses. Voted to discontinue the road from Henry D. Joyce's to the cross-road near M. E. Staples'; also the road from where Benjamin J. Staples' wharf was to the highway, and also the road from Charles W. Kent's to John C. Kent's. The whole amount of tax raised this year was $1,888.21.

1884.

David E. Sprague, Isaiah J. Stockbridge and Oliver L. Joyce, assessors; Oliver L. Joyce, on the school committee. Raised $490 for schools, $350 for current expenses, and $500 for highways. Discontinued the road near 'the head of the harbor. At the State election the vote for governor was: John B. Redman, 35; Frederick Robie, 25; representative to the legislature, William P. Herrick, 56. At the presidential election the democratic electors had 21 votes: the republican, 21; prohibition, 3. A special meeting was held at schoolhouse No. 5, and it was voted to accept the new road laid out at the head of the harbor, and also road south of No. 6 schoolhouse, and to hire $100 to be expended on said roads immediately.

1885.

Joseph W. Staples, Levi B. Joyce and Edmond F. Bridges, assessors; Isaiah J. Stockbridge on the school committee. Raised $485 for schools, $300 for current expenses, and $500 for highways. Voted to discontinue the road from the highway to the old Torrey place, and also the old road eastward of James L. Smith's, abreast the new road laid out. Voted to accept the road laid out from John C. Kent's to Albion W. Smith's field. There were 22 majority in favor of rebuilding county buildings at Ellsworth.

1886.

David E. Sprague, Edmond F. Bridges and Joseph W. Staples, assessors; Alphonso N. Witham, on the school committee. Raised $500 for schools, $350 for current expenses, and $300 for highways. Voted to accept road laid out from Sylvester Morse's to the highway. In the State election the vote for governor was: Clark S. Edwards, 13; Joseph R. Bodwell, 12; for representative to the legislature, Benjamin F. Fifield, 11; Wilmot B. Thurlow, 12.

1887.

Joseph W. Staples, Levi B. Joyce and Benjamin Smith, assessors; Oliver L. Joyce, on the school committee. Raised $500 for schools, $300 for current expenses, and $400 for highways.

1888.

Edmond F. Bridges, Levi B. Joyce and Isaac W. Stinson, assessors; Levi B. Joyce, supervisor of schools. Raised $500 for schools, $300 for current expenses, and $400 for highways. Voted to make a town landing of M. Stinson's wharf, he to be allowed $10 for the use of it.

At the State election the vote for governor was: Edwin C. Burleigh, 19; William L. Putnam, 15; for representative to the legislature, Seth Webb, 22; Frank S. Warren, 15.

1889.

Edmond F. Bridges, Levi B. Joyce and Oliver L. Joyce, assessors; Levi B. Joyce, Oscar S. Erskine and Charles H. Joyce, school committee. Raised $500 for schools, $300 for current expenses, and $400 for highways. Accepted road laid out from Hosea Kent's to John C. Kent's. Voted to unite districts No. 3 and No. 5, and Bradford E. Rowe, Hiram Colomy and Benjamin J. Staples were chosen a committee to locate the schoolhouse for said districts.

1890.

Edmond F. Bridges, Levi B. Joyce and N. T. Morse, assessors; Levi B. Joyce on the school committee. Raised $500 for schools, $400 for highways, $250 for current expenses. At the State election the vote for governor was: Edwin C. Burleigh, 17; William P. Thompson, 34; representative to the legislature, Joseph W. Haskell, 12; Seth Webb, 43.

1891.

Charles H. Joyce, Oliver L. Joyce and Benjamin Smith, assessors; Oliver L. Joyce on the school committee. Raised $500 for schools, $100 for text-books, $500 for highways, and $200 for current expenses. Voted to discontinue the road from the John Smith place to where it joins the road from Herbert Holbrook's; that the assessors examine the road from Herbert Holbrook's place and lay out a road where they think necessary. The assessors are authorized to get a road machine, and if it works satisfactorily to pay for it out of the money raised for roads.

1892.

Edmond F. Bridges, Levi B. Joyce and Joseph W. Staples, assessors; Charles H. Joyce and Isaiah J. Stockbridge, school committee, with Levi B. Joyce chairman. Raised $575 for schools, $50 for text-books, $650 for highways, and $300 for current expenses. At the State election the vote for governor was: Henry B. Cleaves, 21; Charles F. Johnson, 18; Timothy B. Hussey, 1; for representative to the legislature, Wilmot B. Thurlow, 25; Franklin B. Ferguson, 16.

1893.

Isaac W. Stinson, Charles E. Sprague and Frank E. Pettingill, assessors; Levi B. Joyce on the school committee. Raised $75 for text-books, $600 for schools, $550 for highways, $50 on road from David Smith's to Lewis Stanley's; $300 for current expenses. Voted not to divide district No. 4. Voted to apply to the legislature for a town charter, if it can be secured without becoming liable to support the paupers on the adjacent islands.

1894.

Charles E. Sprague, Isaiah J. Stockbridge and Lewis Stanley, assessors; H. W. Small, Isaac W. Stinson and

George Sprague, school committee. H. W. Small was elected supervisor. Raised $600 for schools, $50 for text-books, $450 for current expenses, and $300 for roads. Districts Nos. 1, 3 and 5 were consolidated. Voted to build a two-story schoolhouse for the accommodation of these combined districts. Chose Benjamin Smith, Charles E. Sprague, Hermon W. Small, Dana E. Burns and Benjamin J. Staples as building committee, who shall determine the location of said schoolhouse, and superintend its building.

1895.

There were three meetings this year for the election of municipal officers. The first two were considered void on account of some imformality in the warrants. The first meeting was held March 4, the second March 27; the third at No. 4 schoolhouse on April 18. Chose J. W. Staples, moderator, Levi B. Joyce, clerk. Voted to reconsider the transactions of the two previous meetings, and the officers chosen at these former meetings tendered their resignations. Charles E. Sprague, I. J. Stockbridge and Nelson T. Morse were chosen assessors; I. W. Stinson, treasurer; Fred A. Joyce on the school board; H. W. Small, superintendent of schools; N. T. Morse, collector of taxes. Appropriated $505 for schools, $75 for text-books, $500 for highways, $450 for current expenses, $100 for repairs on schoolhouses.

During the session of the legislature of 1895-6 an act was passed, incorporating into a town Swan's Island and all other islands, the whole or part of which are within three miles from high water mark of said Swan's Island, except Marshall's Island and such islands as are now a part of Long Island plantation. This act was passed, with the provision that this law shall not take effect unless the same is accepted by a majority vote by ballot of the legal voters of Swan's Island, taken at their annual meeting held the first Monday in March, A. D. 1896, an article therefor having been inserted in the warrant calling the meeting. If act is then so accepted, it shall immediately take effect, and the legal voters there present may proceed to elect the usual town officers, and transact any other business as a town of which notice has been given in the warrant calling said meeting of said plantation.

1896.

The annual meeting was held at Atlantic schoolhouse; N. T. Morse was chosen moderator. Voted not to accept the town charter by a vote of 82 to 59. L. B. Joyce was elected clerk; C. H. Joyce, I. J. Stockbridge and Oliver Bowley, assessors; Charles W. Shaw, auditor; I. W. Stinson, treasurer. H. W. Small and Levi B. Joyce on the school board; H. W. Small, superintendent of schools; Fred Turner, road commissioner. Appropriated $505 for schools, $30 for school-books, $300 for highways, $400 for current expenses, and $200 for support of the poor. Voted to pay the balance due on the schoolhouse debt. Accepted the road laid out from near Philip McRae's to S. Morse's.

In State election in September the vote was: For governor, Llewellyn Powers, 22; Melvin P. Frank, 14; representative to the legislature, Stephen B. Thurlow had 32: Dudley W. Fifield, 7. During the session of the legislature of 1896-7 a bill was passed making Swan's Island a town. The limits were the same as in the bill passed by the previous legislature, and contained the following islands: Swan's Island, Orino, Round, Sheep, Finney, Buckle, Crow, Heron, Hat. Hay, Green, Harbor, Scrag, two Bakers, John's and the two Sister islands, which include eighteen out of the twenty-five islands that were originally conveyed to Swan in the Burnt Coat group. The legislature also authorized the new town to collect in all outstanding taxes that had been assessed by the officers of the *de facto* plantation. It also gave authority to any justice of the peace in Hancock county to warn a meeting. This bill, granting a town charter to Swan's Island, was signed by the governor, and became a law March 26, 1897.

1897.

The annual meeting was held March 1, and the usual officers chosen. The question, however, was raised in regard to the legality of the incorporation of the plantation, as no record was to be found of such proceedings, and the legislature did not legalize either the title to a plantation or the transactions that had taken place under the alleged plantation. So a new meeting was warned according to the requirements of the new town charter. The first town meeting was held in No. 4 schoolhouse on April 13. The warrant was issued by Levi B. Joyce, esq., to Llewellyn V. Joyce, directing him to warn a meeting at the above-named place and date, to elect the usual town officers.

The meeting was called to order by L. V. Joyce. Nelson T. Morse was elected moderator; C. E. Sprague, clerk; C. H. Joyce, I. J. Stockbridge and Oliver Bowley, selectmen; George A. Sprague, auditor; I. W. Stinson, treasurer; Isaac W. Stinson, A. C. Smith and E. K. Gott, school board; John Hardy, superintendent of schools; Horace E. Stanley and Fred Turner, road commissioners. Appropriated $505 for schools, $75 for text-books, $400 for roads, $550 for current expenses, $60 for repairs on schoolhouses, and $200 for support of poor. By the death of Congressman Seth L. Milliken, a special election was held June 12 to choose his successor. The vote was: For Edwin C. Burleigh, 24; Frederick W. Plaisted, 4.

1898.

Meeting was held at Atlantic schoolhouse. This year two hundred names appeared on the voting list. The following were the officers chosen: Moderator, C. E. Sprague; clerk, F. F. Morse; selectmen, C. H. Joyce, Oliver Bowley and Linwood E. Joyce; school board, C. E. Sprague, F. F. Morse and Nelson Sprague; superintendent of schools, H. W. Small; auditor, J. W. Staples; road commissioner, David M. Stanley. Appropriated $505 for schools, $700 for town expenses, $500 for highways, $200 for support of poor, $50 for repairs on schoolhouse, $80 for text-books, and $100 for supplies and appliances. Accepted road laid out from John Sprague's to Elias Sprague's.

CHAPTER VIII.

MISCELLANEOUS.

Following are the names of the representatives to the State legislature who have been chosen from Swan's Island. When the first representative was chosen this island was classed with Mt. Desert. The others represented the towns of Deer Isle, Swan's Island and Isle au Haut. The vote given below is for the whole representative district:

Benjamin Stinson was elected in 1837; he received 89 votes; Enoch Spurling, 70.

Benjamin F. Stinson was elected in 1855; he received 162 votes; Solomon Barbour, 134. Mr. Stinson was a candidate for the same office in 1844. His vote in this town was 45; Humphrey Wells, 1. But Mr. Wells received a majority in the district.

Ebenezer Joyce was elected in 1859; he received 135 votes; Franklin Closson, 134.

John Stockbridge was elected in 1867; he received 152 votes; William H. Reed, 74.

Martin V. Babbidge was elected in 1876; he received 268 votes; Augustus O. Gross, 173.

William P. Herrick was elected in 1884; he received 238 votes; Wilmot B. Thurlow, 237.

Charles E. Sprague was elected in 1894; he received 239 votes; Charles L. Knowlton, 155.

The Swan's Island Mutual Fire Insurance Company was organized for the purpose of insuring against loss or damage by fire of buildings and household furniture located on Swan's Island. Afterwards the property on Gott's Island and Orino Island was included. The first meeting to effect an organization was held in the schoolhouse in district No. 2 on January 29, 1893. On February 10 following the signers of the "Articles of Agreement" met and proceeded to elect a board of directors, and adopted a constitution and by-laws. The following was the first board of directors: Frank E. Pettingill, Emery E. Joyce, Edmund F. Bridges, W. Leslie Joyce, Hermon W. Small, Joseph W. Staples, Herbert W. Joyce, James Joyce and Isaac W. Stinson. The board of directors chose Hermon W. Small president; Joseph W. Staples, secretary, and James Joyce, treasurer.

The plan of this insurance was for mutual home protection against loss by fire, at the least expense possible to the policy-holders. The policies ran for a period of seven years, and the policy fees at first were 17, afterwards 25 cents on each $100 insurance. This was just to meet the incidental expenses. The president and secretary together received $1 for the writing of each policy, and the treasurer received 10 per cent. of the gross receipts of these policy fees for his compensation. There were to be no other expenses except loss by fire, when each policyholder was to pay his part of the loss in proportion to the amount for which he was insured. The policy notes were for 10 per cent. of the amount insured. About $25,000 was written the first year. A State charter was issued to this company by the secretary of State on March 23, 1893. The first policies were issued April 18 following.

POSTOFFICES.

For some fifty years after the settlement of this town, there was no postoffice here. Such mail as was received stopped at the postoffice either at Deer Isle or Mount Desert and was brought to this island when a sail-boat chanced to visit those places. This was very inconvenient to the settlers, and often the delivery was long delayed or the mail lost. The first office was established in 1844, and Benjamin Stinson was appointed postmaster. The mail at this time came to the island from Brooklin once a week, and the mail carrier was to be paid by subscription; but as many received little mail, interest in the enterprise soon waned and the burden of carrying the mails fell mostly to the lot of the postmaster. Few newspapers were taken here at that time. Letters were merely folded and secured with sealing-wax — no envelopes were used. Postage was charged according to the distance the letter was sent. It often cost twenty-five cents or more to send a letter to some places even in this country. The postage was collected when the mail was delivered.

Mr. Stinson was succeeded as postmaster by James Joyce, in 1852, and after him Joseph W. Staples was appointed. The mails during the last two appointments, and a long time subsequent, were carried to Tremont.

The receipts of the office were all the department

allowed for the compensation of the postmaster and mail carrier. The pay was so small that great difficulty was experienced in getting a mail carrier, and it was carried so irregularly that a large part of the outgoing letters, from which the revenue came, was sent off by private conveyance. So the receipts of the office were small indeed.

In 1861 Cornelius Wasgatt was appointed postmaster, after which the mails were carried much more regularly. When he moved from the island Mrs. Mary Gott received the appointment. After her resignation Isaac W. Stinson, a grandson of the first Swan's Island postmaster, was appointed, and at the present time the office is held by Capt. William Herrick.

As the town increased in population and the amount of mail became much larger, it proved inconvenient for one office to accommodate the whole island. So, in 1884, an office was established at the eastern side of the island, called Atlantic. Mrs. Durilla Joyce was appointed postmistress. She held the office until 1897, when she was succeeded by Llewellyn V. Joyce. In 1897 a new office was established in what was formerly school district No. 4, and was named Minturn. Mrs. Arwilda Newman was appointed postmistress.

After the mails became somewhat larger than at first, they were carried to Tremont twice a week when the weather would permit a sail-boat to cross the bay. Later they were carried daily. The department established a mail route, and paid the mail carrier. In 1894 this old mail route was discontinued, and a steamboat company contracted to bring the mail daily from Rockland to Old Harbor. This is a much more direct route than when it went by the way of Tremont, and thence by stage to Ellsworth. We have now daily communication with the city, and daily papers are received on the day of publication. In no other way has the improvement been greater than in the management of the mails, which is so vital to the business interest of any community.

CHURCHES.

The early settlers here were a religious people, and, although they had no pastor or place for public worship, they made up for this lack of privilege by holding Sunday service in some dwelling-house, where one of the company performed the service usual in those times by reading a sermon. Mid-week prayer meetings were also held. These services were attended by the people from the different sections of the whole island, and on pleasant days they would come from the neighboring islands. Most of the first settlers were of the Congregational denomination, but that church never formed an organization.

A Baptist preacher came here about the year 1814, and conducted a series of revival meetings; as a result, quite a number joined the church of that denomination. In 1817 a Baptist society was organized in that part of the town now known as Atlantic. According to the minutes of the Baptist association, held in Sedgwick Oct. 12, 1820, the Swan's Island church was taken into the association. Rev. Bryant Lennan, a licensed preacher, and Joshua

Staples represented this church at this association. They reported the membership at that time to be twenty-three.

In 1821 the Swan's Island church was represented at the Baptist association held at Surry by Rev. Bryant Lennan and Courtney Babbidge. Two members had been excluded during the year, leaving twenty-one members in good standing. In the association held in Addison in 1822, this church was not represented. Rev. Bryant Lennan was ordained during the year. This church was represented at the association held in Brooksville in 1823, by Rev. Bryant Lennan, Deacon James Joyce and Joshua Staples. The membership was the same as last reported. In 1824 the association that met at Bluehill reported this church membership to have been increased by the baptism of thirteen candidates, making the total membership this year thirty-four. This year the church was represented by Rev. Mr. Lennan, Courtney Babbidge and Ebenezer Joyce.

Mr. Lennan was connected with the church for many years. He is said to have been a faithful pastor and was considered a good preacher. He finally returned to Hampden, his native town. After some fifteen years Mr. Lennan returned and preached a few years, after which I find no further record of him.

Rev. Theophilus Batchelder preached alternately here and at Deer Isle for several years. Rev. Benjamin F. Stinson preached here a great deal at different times. He did faithful service and was much loved and respected by the church here. After the schoolhouse was built at the eastern side of the island services were held there. Services in those times were very long. After a sermon of an hour, a short intermission would be taken, after which a second sermon was preached.

Rev. Daniel Dodge preached a part of the year 1838. Ebenezer Joyce was chosen deacon. The conference delegates were James Joyce, John Stockbridge and Ebenezer Joyce. In 1840 quite a revival took place under the pastorate of Rev. Samuel Macomber. Asa Joyce, Sally Stockbridge, John Cook and Jane Morey were taken into the church. In 1842 26 more joined. From 1843-5 meetings were held more or less regularly by Elder St. Clair, Carey or Dunham. From 1847 to 1850 the preachers were Revs. Messrs. Macomber, Hall and Pendleton. During the latter years several more were taken into the church.

For the next few years the interest of the church members gradually declined. On July 14, 1857, a church meeting was called. Those present were Rebecca Staples, Betsey Staples, Sally Morey, Catherine Joyce, Rosalana Morey, Nancy Morey, Polly Babbidge, Ebenezer Joyce. James Joyce, John Stockbridge, Joseph S. Babbidge and Elias Morey. They made an effort to establish the meetings again. As a result Revs. Samuel Macomber and Theophilus Batchelder preached a part of the year.

The following were the members of the Baptist church on April 6, 1867: James Joyce, Ebenezer Joyce, Joseph S. Babbidge, Joseph R. Torrey, Asa Joyce, Hezekiah Morey, Benjamin Stockbridge, Samuel Stockbridge,

Isaiah B. Joyce, Eben S. Joyce, Henry D. Joyce, James Joyce, jr., Benjamin F. Staples, Simeon R. Staples, William A. Joyce, Otis Morey, Rebecca Staples, Mary Trask, Polly Babbidge, James Joyce, Catherine Joyce, Olive Torrey, Roxana Torrey, Isabel S. Joyce, Jane J. Joyce, Martha Torrey, Harriet Staples, Sophronia Staples, Louisa Staples, Nancy Morey, Susan Reed and Sally Morey—thirty-two in all.

On April 7, 1857, nine more joined : on the next Sunday fifteen more joined — making the total membership at this time fifty-six. On May 16, 1886, Rev. C. E. Harden baptized nine persons. The following Sunday Rev. Gideon Mayo baptized five.

Among the preachers during the previous twenty years were Revs. B. F. Stinson, N. G. French, C. E. Harden, Mr. Pierce and Gideon Mayo.

In 1886-9 Rev. George D. B. Pepper, D. D., president of Colby university, preached here during the summer. During 1888-9 Rev. William H. Hall preached here. From 1888 to 1891 thirty-one persons joined the church. The membership had now increased to over seventy.

A church was built by this society in 1883 at a cost of $3,500. In 1890 and 1891 Rev. W. H. Hall conducted a series of revival meetings, and a large number was added to the church membership. Rev. J. Frank Jones was the pastor in 1891-2. In 1894 Rev. S. O. Whitten came and preached three years. A two-story parsonage was built in 1891 at a cost of $1,400. At present there is no settled pastor, and the church membership has fallen to fifty-nine.

The Methodist society was organized in 1834. The first preacher of that denomination here was Rev. Asa Wasgatt. Soon after Rev. Mr. Douglass came here from Bar Harbor, and baptized several candidates. In 1859 Rev. Benjamin F. Stinson, of this town, entered the ministry, and for the twenty-eight years that he preached, much of the time was devoted to the church in his native town. In 1860 Mr. Stinson preached in Tremont; '61, '62 in Deer Isle; '63, '64 in Franklin; '65, '66 in Columbia; '67, '69 in Tremont; '70, '71 in Harrington; '73 in South Deer Isle; '75 and until his death in 1887 he preached at Tremont and this town on alternate Sundays.

Rev. John A. Oakes came in 1861, and preached two years. The services were held during this time at the Center schoolhouse. The other preachers were Rev. A. Plummer; Mr. Caldwell, who stayed here two years. He was followed by Rev. Theophilus Batchelder, who also preached in the Baptist church. For several years after this there was no regular preacher. In 1882 Rev. Israel Hathaway came and preached about two years until his death. He was followed by Elder Roberts. George A. Fuller and I. B. Conley.

In 1888 a church was built at a cost of $2,500. Since then a pastor has been regularly employed. They have been Revs. Wesley Haskell, Samuel E. Dunham, George M. Bailey, Horace Haskell, Andrew J. Turner, Lester

McCalf, Chester Butterfield. The present pastor is Rev. John L. Pinkerton. The present membership is thirty.

The Advent society has been organized for some years, and has quite a large number of church members. A church was erected in 1893. There is no regular pastor, but one is furnished more or less regularly, and when without a pastor, the services are conducted by a member. Their church seems to be in a vigorous and growing condition.

CONCLUSION.

This work has extended far beyond my original intentions. It has covered, I think, nearly everything likely to be of public interest since the discovery of this island. As stated elsewhere, errors will undoubtedly appear. The author knew of but few of the people or events personally; he has had to depend, in some parts, almost wholly upon the memory of aged people. But the best information gleaned from these sources has been faithfully recorded.

I have been five years in collecting these records, much of which, had it not been secured during the lifetime of the oldest residents, would have been lost beyond recovery.

The descendants of many of the early families who lived here are scattered among different towns and states, and it has required a great deal of patient toil to find them all, and collect their family history, so as to make their record complete.

To the many who have so kindly furnished the material for this work, the author extends his thanks, and to them he is greatly indebted.

INDEX OF FIRST SETTLERS.

	PAGE.
Adams, John	142
Babbidge, Courtney	96
Barbour, Solomon	155
Benson, Jephtha	138
Billings, Enoch	120
Bridges, Moses	156
Carpenter, Richard	75
Clark, Samuel C.	48
Colomy, Thomas	121
Conary, Israel	134
Cook, John	99
Davis, William	75
Dunbar, Thomas	126
Fife, William	137
Finney, John	107
Gott, Daniel	163
Gott, Peter	108
Grindle, Joshua	70
Hamblen, Daniel	173
Hardy, Silas	141
Herrick, Kimball	123
Holbrook, Abram	152
Joyce, James	88
Kempton, Seth	144
Kempton, Samuel	71
Kempton, Zachariah	144
Kench, Thomas	59

Kent, Samuel	124
Kiff, Alexander	153
Lane, Hardy	145
Lane, Oliver	145
Lennan, Rev. Bryant	102
Mitchell, Robert	146
Morey, Elias, jr.	100
Nutter, Alexander	72
Nutter, William	128
Prince, Joseph	23
Reed, Jacob S.	150
Remick, Joseph	86
Rich, John	73
Richardson, James	172
Richardson, Stephen	173
Richardson, Thomas	173
Sadler, Joshua	128
Sadler, Thomas	130
Sadler, Moses	132
Smith, David	61
Sprague, James T.	132
Stanley, William	134
Staples, Moses	75
Stewart, Cushing	114
Stinson, Benjamin	115
Stockbridge, John	103
Swan, Col. James	44
Swan, James Keadie	55
Toothaker, Joseph	70
Torrey, Levi	94
Trask, Joshua S.	149
Valentine, John	121

www.ingramcontent.com/pod-product-compliance
Lightning Source LLC
Chambersburg PA
CBHW031733230426
43669CB00007B/337